RELIGION IN THE MAKING

A LIVING AGE BOOK

RELIGION
IN THE MAKING

Alfred North Whitehead

Meridian Books

THE WORLD PUBLISHING COMPANY
Cleveland and New York

A LIVING AGE BOOK (MERIDIAN)

Published by The World Publishing Company
2231 West 110th Street, Cleveland 2, Ohio
First Meridian printing January 1960
Sixth Printing November 1966
Library of Congress Catalog Card Number: 60-6736
Printed in the United States of America   6FDI1166

To E. W.

This book consists of four lectures on religion delivered in King's Chapel, Boston, during February, 1926. The train of thought which was applied to science in my Lowell Lectures of the previous year, since published under the title, *Science and the Modern World*, is here applied to religion. The two books are independent, but it is inevitable that to some extent they elucidate each other by showing the same way of thought in different applications.

The aim of the lectures was to give a concise analysis of the various factors in human nature which go to form a religion, to exhibit the inevitable transformation of religion with the transformation of knowledge, and more especially to direct attention to the foundation of religion on our apprehension of those permanent elements by reason of which there is a stable order in the world, permanent elements apart from which there could be no changing world.

A. N. W.

Harvard University
   March 13, 1926

CONTENTS

PREFACE   7

I: RELIGION IN HISTORY
    1. Religion Defined   13
    2. The Emergence of Religion   18
    3. Ritual and Emotion   20
    4. Belief   23
    5. Rationalism   28
    6. The Ascent of Man   37
    7. The Final Contrast   40

II: RELIGION AND DOGMA
    1. The Religious Consciousness in History   47
    2. The Description of Religious Experience   57
    3. God   66
    4. The Quest of God   72

III: BODY AND SPIRIT
    1. Religion and Metaphysics   81

2. The Contribution of Religion to
   Metaphysics   84
3. A Metaphysical Description   86
4. God and the Moral Order   91
5. Value and the Purpose of God   97
6. Body and Mind   102
7. The Creative Process   107

IV: TRUTH AND CRITICISM
1. The Development of Dogma   119
2. Experience and Expression   127
3. The Three Traditions   134
4. The Nature of God   143
5. Conclusion   151

I: RELIGION IN HISTORY

It is my purpose in the four lectures of this course to consider the type of justification which is available for belief in doctrines of religion. This is a question which in some new form challenges each generation. It is the peculiarity of religion that humanity is always shifting its attitude towards it.

The contrast between religion and the elementary truths of arithmetic makes my meaning clear. Ages ago the simple arithmetical doctrines dawned on the human mind, and throughout history the unquestioned dogma that two and three make five reigned whenever it has been relevant. We all know what this doctrine means, and its history is of no importance for its elucidation.

But we have the gravest doubt as to what

religion means so far as doctrine is concerned. There is no agreement as to the definition of religion in its most general sense, including true and false religion; nor is there any agreement as to the valid religious beliefs, nor even as to what we mean by the truth of religion. It is for this reason that some consideration of religion as an unquestioned factor throughout the long stretch of human history is necessary to secure the relevance of any discussion of its general principles.

There is yet another contrast. What is generally disputed is doubtful, and what is doubtful is relatively unimportant—other things being equal. I am speaking of general truths. We avoid guiding our actions by general principles which are entirely unsettled. If we do not know what number is the product of 69 and 67, we defer any action presupposing the answer, till we have found out. This little arithmetical puzzle can be put aside till it is settled, and it is capable of definite settlement with adequate trouble.

But as between religion and arithmetic, other things are not equal. You *use* arithmetic, but you *are* religious. Arithmetic of course enters into your nature, so far as that nature involves a multiplicity of things. But it is there as a necessary condition, and not as a transforming agency. No one is invariably "justified" by his faith in the multiplication table. But in some sense or other, justification is the basis of all religion. Your character is developed according to your faith. This is the primary religious truth from which no one can escape. Religion is force of belief cleansing the inward parts. For this reason the primary religious virtue is sincerity, a penetrating sincerity.

A religion, on its doctrinal side, can thus be defined as a system of general truths which have the effect of transforming character when they are sincerely held and vividly apprehended.

In the long run your character and your conduct of life depend upon your intimate convictions. Life is an internal fact for its own sake, before it is an external fact relating itself to others. The conduct of external life is conditioned by environment, but it receives its final quality, on which its worth depends, from the internal life which is the

self-realization of existence. Religion is the
art and the theory of the internal life of man,
so far as it depends on the man himself and on
what is permanent in the nature of things.

This doctrine is the direct negation of the
theory that religion is primarily a social fact.
Social facts are of great importance to religion, because there is no such thing as absolutely independent existence. You cannot abstract society from man; most psychology is
herd-psychology. But all collective emotions
leave untouched the awful ultimate fact,
which is the human being, consciously alone
with itself, for its own sake.

Religion is what the individual does with
his own solitariness. It runs through three
stages, if it evolves to its final satisfaction. It
is the transition from God the void to God
the enemy, and from God the enemy to God
the companion.

Thus religion is solitariness; and if you are
never solitary, you are never religious. Collective enthusiasms, revivals, institutions,
churches, rituals, bibles, codes of behaviour,
are the trappings of religion, its passing forms.

They may be useful, or harmful; they may be authoritatively ordained, or merely temporary expedients. But the end of religion is beyond all this.

Accordingly, what should emerge from religion is individual worth of character. But worth is positive or negative, good or bad. Religion is by no means necessarily good. It may be very evil. The fact of evil, interwoven with the texture of the world, shows that in the nature of things there remains effectiveness for degradation. In your religious experience the God with whom you have made terms may be the God of destruction, the God who leaves in his wake the loss of the greater reality.

In considering religion, we should not be obsessed by the idea of its necessary goodness. This is a dangerous delusion. The point to notice is its transcendent importance; and the fact of this importance is abundantly made evident by the appeal to history.

2. THE EMERGENCE OF RELIGION

Religion, so far as it receives external expression in human history, exhibits four factors or sides of itself. These factors are ritual, emotion, belief, rationalization. There is definite organized procedure, which is ritual: there are definite types of emotional expression: there are definitely expressed beliefs: and there is the adjustment of these beliefs into a system, internally coherent and coherent with other beliefs.

But all these four factors are not of equal influence throughout all historical epochs. The religious idea emerged gradually into human life, at first barely disengaged from other human interests. The order of the emergence of these factors was in the inverse order of the depth of their religious importance: first ritual, then emotion, then belief, then rationalization.

The dawn of these religious stages is gradual. It consists in an increase of emphasis. Perhaps it is untrue to affirm that the later factors are ever wholly absent. But certainly, when we go far enough back, belief and rationalization are completely negligible, and emotion is merely a secondary result of ritual. Then emotion takes the lead, and the ritual is for the emotion which it generates. Belief then makes its appearance as explanatory of the complex of ritual and emotion, and in this appearance of belief we may discern the germ of rationalization.

It is not until belief and rationalization are well established that solitariness is discernible as constituting the heart of religious importance. The great religious conceptions which haunt the imaginations of civilized mankind are scenes of solitariness: Prometheus chained to his rock, Mahomet brooding in the desert, the meditations of the Buddha, the solitary Man on the Cross. It belongs to the depth of the religious spirit to have felt forsaken, even by God.

3. RITUAL AND EMOTION

Ritual goes back beyond the dawn of history. It can be discerned in the animals, in their individual habits and still more in their collective evolutions. Ritual may be defined as the habitual performance of definite actions which have no direct relevance to the preservation of the physical organisms of the actors.

Flocks of birds perform their ritual evolutions in the sky. In Europe rooks and starlings are notable examples of this fact. Ritual is the primitive outcome of superfluous energy and leisure. It exemplifies the tendency of living bodies to repeat their own actions. Thus the actions necessary in hunting for food, or in other useful pursuits, are repeated for their own sakes; and their repetition also repeats the joy of exercise and the emotion of success.

In this way emotion waits upon ritual; and then ritual is repeated and elaborated for the sake of its attendant emotions. Mankind became artists in ritual. It was a tremendous discovery—how to excite emotions for their own sake, apart from some imperious biological necessity. But emotions sensitize the organism. Thus the unintended effect was produced of sensitizing the human organism in a variety of ways diverse from what would have been produced by the necessary work of life.

Mankind was started upon its adventures of curiosity and of feeling.

It is evident that, according to this account, religion and play have the same origin in ritual. This is because ritual is the stimulus to emotion, and an habitual ritual may diverge into religion or into play, according to the quality of the emotion excited. Even in comparatively modern times, among the Greeks of the fifth century before Christ, the Olympic Games were tinged with religion, and the Dionysiac festival in Attica ended with a comic drama. Also in the modern world, a holy day and a holiday are kindred notions.

Ritual is not the only way of artificially stimulating emotion. Drugs are equally effective. Luckily the range of drugs at the command of primitive races was limited. But there is ample evidence of the religious use of drugs in conjunction with the religious use of ritual. For example Athenæus tells us that among the Persians it was the religious duty of the King, once a year, at some stated festival in honour of Mithras, to appear in the temple intoxicated.* A relic of the religious awe at intoxication is the use of wine in the Communion service. It is an example of the upward trend of ritual by which a widespread association of thought is elevated into a great symbolism, divested of its primitive grossness.

In this primitive phase of religion, dominated by ritual and emotion, we are dealing with essentially social phenomena. Ritual is more impressive, and emotion more active, when a whole society is concerned in the same ritual and the same emotion. Accordingly, a collective ritual and a collective emotion take their places as one of the binding forces of

* Cf. *The Deipnosophistæ of Athenæus*, Book X. I am indebted to my friend Professor J. H. Woods for this reference.

savage tribes. They represent the first faint glimmerings of the life of the spirit raised beyond concentration upon the task of supplying animal necessities. Conversely, religion in its decay sinks back into sociability.

4. BELIEF

Mere ritual and emotion cannot maintain themselves untouched by intellectuality. Also the abstract idea of maintaining the ritual for the sake of the emotion, though it may express the truth about the subconscious psychology of primitive races, is far too abstract to enter into their conscious thoughts. A myth satisfies the demands of incipient rationality. Men found themselves practising various rituals, and found the rituals generating emotions. The myth explains the purpose both of the ritual and of the emotion. It is the product of the vivid fancy of primitive men in an unfathomed world.

To primitive man, and to ourselves on our

primitive side, the universe is not so much unfathomable as unfathomed—by this I mean undiscriminated, unanalyzed. It is not a complex of definite unexplained happenings, but a dim background shot across by isolated vivid effects charged with emotional excitements. The very presuppositions of a coherent rationalism are absent. Such a rationalism presupposes a complex of definite facts whose interconnections are sought. But the prior stage is a background of indefiniteness relieved by vivid acts of definition, inherently isolated. One exception must be made in favour of the routine of tribal necessities which are taken for granted. But what lies beyond the routine of life is in general void of definition; and when it is vivid, it is disconnected.

The myth which meets the ritual is some exceptional vivid fancy, or recollection of some actual vivid fact—probably distorted in remembrance—which appears not only as explanatory both of ritual and emotion, but also as generative of emotion when conjoined with the ritual. Thus the myth not only explains but reinforces the hidden purpose of the ritual, which is emotion.

Then rituals and emotions and myths reciprocally interact; and the myths have various grades of relationship to actual fact, and have various grades of symbolic truth as being representative of large ideas only to be apprehended in some parable. Also in some cases the myth precedes the ritual. But there is the general fact that ritualism precedes mythology. For we can observe ritualism even among animals, and presumably they are destitute of a mythology.

A myth will involve special attention to some persons or to some things, real or imaginary. Thus in a sense, the ritual, as performed in conjunction with the explanatory purpose of the myth, is the primitive worship of the hero-person or the hero-thing. But there can be very little disinterested worship among primitive folk—even less than now, if possible. Accordingly, the belief in the myth will involve the belief that something is to be got out of him or it, or that something is to be averted in respect to the evil to be feared from him or it. Thus incantation, prayer, praise, and ritual absorption of the hero deity emerge.

If the hero be a person, we call the ritual, with its myth, "religion"; if the hero be a thing, we call it "magic." In religion we induce, in magic we compel. The important difference between magic and religion is that magic is unprogressive and religion sometimes is progressive; except in so far as science can be traced back to the progress of magic.

Religion, in this stage of belief, marks a new formative agent in the ascent of man. For just as ritual encouraged *emotion* beyond the mere response to practical necessities, so religion in this further stage begets *thoughts* divorced from the mere battling with the pressure of circumstances. Imagination secured in it a machinery for its development; thought has been thereby led beyond the immediate objects in sight. Its concepts may in these early stages be crude and horrible; but they have the supreme virtue of being concepts of objects beyond immediate sense and perception.

This is the stage of uncoördinated beliefs.

So far as this is the dominant phase there can be a curious tolerance, in that one cult does not war upon another cult. Since there is a minimum of coördination, there is room for all. But religion is still a thoroughly social phenomenon. The cult includes the tribe, or at least it includes some well-defined body of persons within the social organism. You may not desert your own cults, but there need be no clash between cults. In the higher stages of such a religion there are tribal gods, or many gods within a tribe, with the loosest coördination of cults and myths.

Though religion can be a source of progress, it need not be so, especially when its dominant feature is this stage of uncriticized belief. It is easy for a tribe to stabilize its ritual and its myths, and there need be no external spur to progress. In fact, this is the stage of religious evolution in which the masses of semi-civilized humanity have halted—the stage of satisfactory ritual and of satisfied belief without impulse towards higher things. Such religion satisfies the pragmatic test: It works, and thereby claims that it be awarded the prize for truth.

5. RATIONALISM

The age of martyrs dawns with the coming
of rationalism. The antecedent phases of religion had been essentially sociable. Many
were called, and all were chosen. The final
phase introduces the note of solitariness:
"Strait is the gate, and narrow is the way . . .
and few there be that find it." When a modern
religion forgets this saying, it is suffering from
an atavistic relapse into primitive barbarism.
It is appealing to the psychology of the herd,
away from the intuitions of the few.

The religious epoch which we are now
considering is very modern. Its past duration
is of the order of six thousand years. Of
course exact dates do not count; you can extend the epoch further back into the past in
order to include some faint anticipatory
movement, or you can contract its duration
so as to exclude flourishing survivals of the

earlier phase. The movement has extended over all the civilized races of Asia and Europe. In the past Asia has proved the most fertile in ideas, but within the last two thousand years Europe has given the movement a new aspect. It is to be noted that the two most perfect examples of rationalistic religions have flourished chiefly in countries foreign to the races among which they had their origin.

The Bible is by far the most complete account of the coming of rationalism into religion, based on the earliest documents available. Viewed as such an account, it is only relevant to the region between the Tigris and the Nile. It exhibits the note of progressive solitariness in the religious idea: first, types of thought generally prevalent; then protesting prophets, isolated figures of denunciation and exhortation stirring the Jewish nation; then one man, with twelve disciples, who met with almost complete national rejection; then the adaptation for popular survival of this latter doctrine by another man who, very significantly, had no first-hand contact with the original teaching. In his hands, something was added and something was lost; but fortunately the Gospels also survive.

It is evident that I have drawn attention to the span of six thousand years because, in addition to being reasonable when we have regard to all the evidence, it corresponds to the chronology of the Bible. We—in Europe and America—are the heirs of the religious movements depicted in that collection of books. Discussion on the methods of religion and their justification must, in order to be relevant, base itself upon the Bible for illustration. We must remember, however, that Buddhism and Mahometanism, among others, must also be included in the scope of general statements, even if they are not explicitly referred to.

Rational religion is religion whose beliefs and rituals have been reorganized with the aim of making it the central element in a coherent ordering of life—an ordering which shall be coherent both in respect to the elucidation of thought, and in respect to the direction of conduct towards a unified purpose commanding ethical approval.

The peculiar position of religion is that it stands between abstract metaphysics and the particular principles applying to only some among the experiences of life. The relevance of its concepts can only be distinctly discerned in moments of insight, and then, for many of us, only after suggestion from without. Hence religion bases itself primarily upon a small selection from the common experiences of the race. On this side, religion ranges itself as one among other specialized interests of mankind whose truths are of limited validity. But on its other side, religion claims that its concepts, though derived primarily from special experiences, are yet of universal validity, to be applied by faith to the ordering of all experience.

Rational religion appeals to the direct intuition of special occasions, and to the elucidatory power of its concepts for all occasions. It arises from that which is special, but it extends to what is general. The doctrines of rational religion aim at being that metaphysics which can be derived from the supernormal experience of mankind in its moments of finest insight. Theoretically, rational re-

ligion could have arisen in complete independence of the antecedent social religions of
ritual and mythical belief. Before the historical sense had established itself, that was the
way in which the apologetic theologians
tended to exhibit the origins of their respective religions. But the general history of religion, and in particular that portion of its
history contained in the Bible, decisively
negatives that view. Rational religion
emerged as a gradual transformation of the
preëxisting religious forms. Finally, the old
forms could no longer contain the new ideas,
and the modern religions of civilization are
traceable to definite crises in this process of
development. But the development was not
then ended; it had only acquired more suitable forms for self-expression.

The emergence of rational religion was
strictly conditioned by the general progress
of the races in which it arose. It had to wait
for the development in human consciousness
of the relevant general ideas and of the relevant ethical intuitions. It required that such
ideas should not merely be casually entertained by isolated individuals, but that they

should be stabilized in recognizable forms of expression, so as to be recalled and communicated. You can only speak of mercy among a people who, in some respects, are already merciful.

A language is not a universal mode of expressing all ideas whatsoever. It is a limited mode of expressing such ideas as have been frequently entertained, and urgently needed, by the group of human beings who developed that mode of speech. It is only during a comparatively short period of human history that there has existed any language with an adequate stock of general terms. Such general terms require a permanent literature to define them by their mode of employment.

The result is that the free handling of general ideas is a late acquirement. I am not maintaining that the brains of men were inadequate for the task. The point is that it took ages for them to develop first the appliances and then the habits which made generality of thought possible and prevalent. For ages, existing languages must have been ready for development. If men had been in contact with a superior race, either personally or by a survival of their literature, a process which requires scores or even hundreds of generations might have been antedated, so as to have been effected almost at once. Such, in fact, was the later history of the development of the races of Northern Europe. Again, a social system which encourages developments of thought can procure the advent. This is the way in which the result was first obtained. Society and language grew together.

The influence of the antecedent type of religion, ceremonial, mythical, and sociable, has been great; and the estimates as to its value diverse. During the thousand years preceding the Christian era, there was a peculiarly intense struggle on the part of rationalism to transform the more primitive type. The issue was a new synthesis which, in the forms of the various great religions, has lasted to the present day. A rational generality was introduced into the religious ideas; and the myth, when retained, was reorganized with the intention of making it an account of verifiable historical circumstances which exemplified the general ideas with adequate perfection.

Thus rational criticism was admitted in principle. The appeal was from the tribal custom to the direct individual intuition, ethical, metaphysical, or logical: "For I desired mercy, and not sacrifice; and the knowledge of God more than burnt offerings," are words which Hosea ascribes to Jehovah; and he thereby employs the principles of individual criticism of tribal custom, and bases it upon direct ethical intuition.

In this way the religions evolved towards more individualistic forms, shedding their exclusively communal aspect. The individual became the religious unit in the place of the community; the tribal dance lost its importance compared to the individual prayer; and, for the few, the individual prayer merged into justification through individual insight.

So to-day it is not France which goes to heaven, but individual Frenchmen; and it is not China which attains nirvana, but Chinamen.

During this epoch of struggle—as in most religious struggles—the judgments passed by the innovators on the less-developed religious forms were very severe. The condemnation of idolatry pervades the Bible; and there are traces of a recoil which go further: "I hate, I despise your feast days," writes Amos, speaking in the name of Jehovah.

Such criticism is wanted. Indeed history, down to the present day, is a melancholy record of the horrors which can attend religion: human sacrifice, and in particular the slaughter of children, cannibalism, sensual orgies, abject superstition, hatred as between races, the maintenance of degrading customs, hysteria, bigotry, can all be laid at its charge. Religion is the last refuge of human savagery. The uncritical association of religion with goodness is directly negatived by plain facts. Religion can be, and has been, the main instrument for progress. But if we survey the whole race, we must pronounce that generally it has not been so: "Many are called, but few are chosen."

6. THE ASCENT OF MAN

At different epochs in history new factors emerge and successively assume decisive importance in their influence on the ascent, or the descent, of races of mankind. Within the millennium preceding the birth of Christ, the communal religions were ceasing to be engines of progress. On the whole, they had served humanity well. By their agency, the sense of social unity and of social responsibility had been quickened. The common cult gave expression to the emotion of being a hundred per cent tribal. The explicit emotions of a life finding its interest in activities not directed to its own preservation were fostered by them. Also they produced concrete beliefs which embodied, however waveringly, the justification for these emotions.

But at a certain stage in history, though still elements in the preservation of the social structure, they ceased to be engines of progress. Their work was done.

They were salving the old virtues which had made the race the great society that it had been, and were not straining forward towards the new virtues to make the common life the City of God that it should be. They were religions of the average, and the average is at war with the ideal.

Human thought had broken through the limited horizon of the one social structure. The world as a whole entered into the explicit consciousness. The facility for individual wandering in comparative safety produced this enlargement of thought. A tribe which is wandering as a unit amid dangers may pick up new ideas, but it will strengthen its sense of tribal unity in the face of a hostile environment.

But an individual who travels meets strangers on terms of kindliness. He returns home, and in his person and by his example promotes the habit of thinking dispassionately beyond the tribe. The history of rational religion is full of tales of disengagement from the immediate social routine. If we keep to the Bible: Abraham wandered, the Jews were carried off to Babylon and after two generations were allowed to return peacefully, St. Paul's conversion was on a journey, and his theology was elaborated amid travels. This millennium was an age of travel; among the Greeks, Herodotus, Thucydides, Plato, Xenophon, Aristotle, exemplify their times. The great empires and trading facilities made travelling easy; everyone travelled and found the world fresh and new. A world-consciousness was produced.

In India and China the growth of a world-consciousness was different in its details, but in its essence depended on the same factors. Individuals were disengaged from their immediate social setting in ways which promoted thought.

Now, so far as concerns religion, the distinction of a world-consciousness as contrasted with a social consciousness is the change of emphasis in the concept of rightness. A social consciousness concerns people whom you know and love individually. Hence, rightness is mixed up with the notion of preservation. Conduct is right which will lead some god to protect you; and it is wrong if it stirs some irascible being to compass your destruction. Such religion is a branch of diplomacy. But a world-consciousness is more disengaged. It rises to the conception of an essential rightness of things. The individuals are indifferent, because unknown. The new, and almost profane, concept of the goodness of God replaces the older emphasis on the will of God. In a communal religion you study the will of God in order that He may preserve you; in a purified religion, rationalized under the influence of the world-concept, you study his goodness in order to be like him. It is the difference between the enemy you conciliate and the companion whom you imitate.

7. THE FINAL CONTRAST

A survey of religious history has disclosed that the coming of rational religion is the consequence of the growth of a world-consciousness. The later phases of the antecedent communal type of religion are dominated by the conscious reaction of human nature to the social organization in which it finds itself. Such reaction is partly emotion clothing itself in belief and ritual, and partly reason justifying practice by the test of social preservation. Rational religion is the wider conscious reaction of men to the universe in which they find themselves.

Communal religion broadened itself to the verge of rationalism. In its last stages in the Western World we find the religion of the Roman Empire, in which the widest possible view of the social structure is adopted. The cult of the Empire was the sort of religion which might be constructed to-day by the Law School of a University, laudably impressed by the notion that mere penal repression is not the way to avert a crime wave. Indeed, if we study the mentality of the Emperor Augustus and of the men who surrounded him, this is not far off from the true description of its final step in evolution.

Another type of modified communal religion was reached by the Jews. Their religion embodied general ideas as to the nature of things which were entirely expressed in terms of their relevance to the Jewish race. This compromise was very effective, but very unstable. It is a type of religious settlement to which communities are always reverting. In the modern world it is the religion of emotional statesmen, captains of industry, and social reformers. In the case of the Jews the crises to which it led were the birth of Christianity, and the forcible dispersion of the Jews by the military might of Rome. The same type of religion in our generation was one of the factors which led to the great war. It leads to the morbid exaggeration of national self-consciousness. It lacks the element of quietism. Generality is the salt of religion.

When Christianity had established itself throughout the Roman Empire and its neighbourhood, there were before the world two main rational religions, Buddhism and Christianity. There were, of course, many rivals to both of them in their respective regions; but if we have regard to clarity of idea, generality of thought, moral respectability, survival power, and width of extension over the world, then for their combination of all these qualities these religions stood out beyond their competitors. Later their position was challenged by the Mahometans. But even to-day, the two Catholic religions of civilization are Christianity and Buddhism, and—if we are to judge by the comparison of their position now with what it has been—both of them are in decay. They have lost their ancient hold upon the world.

II: RELIGION AND DOGMA

I. THE RELIGIOUS CONSCIOUSNESS IN HISTORY

The great rational religions are the outcome of the emergence of a religious consciousness which is universal, as distinguished from tribal, or even social. Because it is universal, it introduces the note of solitariness. Religion is what the individual does with his solitariness.

The reason of this connection between universality and solitariness is that universality is a disconnection from immediate surroundings. It is an endeavour to find something permanent and intelligible by which to interpret the confusion of immediate detail.

This element of detachment in religion is more particularly exhibited in the great reflective books of the Old Testament. In this group of books we find a conscious search after general principles. In other books, current ideas are assumed and are applied to the troubles of what was then the immediate present. Such books exemplify the state of thought of their times as in controversy, but they do not exhibit a process of reflective formation.

In the reflective books the effort is not to reform society, or even to express religious emotion. There is a self-conscious endeavour to apprehend some general principles.

In the book of Job we find the picture of a man suffering from an almost fantastic array of the evils characteristic of his times. He is tearing to pieces the sophism that all is for the best in the best of possible worlds, and that the justice of God is beautifully evident in everything that happens. The essence of the book of Job is the contrast of a general principle, or dogma, and the particular circumstances to which it should apply. There is also throughout the book the undercurrent of fear lest an old-fashioned tribal god might take offense at this rational criticism.

No religion which faces facts can minimize the evil in the world, not merely the moral evil, but the pain and the suffering. The book of Job is the revolt against the facile solution, so esteemed by fortunate people, that the sufferer is the evil person.

Both the great religions, Christianity and Buddhism, have their separate set of dogmas which deal with this great question. It is in respect to the problem of evil that one great divergence between them exists. Buddhism finds evil essential in the very nature of the world of physical and emotional experience. The wisdom which it inculcates is, therefore, so to conduct life as to gain a release from the individual personality which is the vehicle for such experience. The Gospel which it preaches is the method by which this release can be obtained.

One metaphysical fact about the nature of things which it presupposes is that this release is not to be obtained by mere physical death. Buddhism is the most colossal example in history of applied metaphysics.

Christianity took the opposite road. It has always been a religion seeking a metaphysic, in contrast to Buddhism which is a metaphysic generating a religion. The defect of a metaphysical system is the very fact that it is a neat little system of thought, which thereby over-simplifies its expression of the world. Christianity has, in its historical development, struggled with another difficulty, namely, the fact that it has no clear-cut separation from the crude fancies of the older tribal religions.

But Christianity has one advantage. It is difficult to develop Buddhism, because Buddhism starts with a clear metaphysical notion and with the doctrines which flow from it. Christianity has retained the easy power of development. It starts with a tremendous notion about the world. But this notion is not derived from a metaphysical doctrine, but from our comprehension of the sayings and actions of certain supreme lives. It is the genius of the religion to point at the facts and ask for their systematic interpretation. In the Sermon on the Mount, in the Parables, and in their accounts of Christ, the Gospels exhibit a tremendous fact. The doctrine may, or may not, lie on the surface. But what is primary is the religious fact. The Buddha left a tremendous doctrine. The historical facts about him are subsidiary to the doctrine.

In respect to its treatment of evil, Christianity is, therefore, less clear in its metaphysical ideas, but more inclusive of the facts. In the first place, it admits the evil as inherent throughout the world. But it holds that such evil is not the necessary outcome of the very fact of individual personality. It derives the evil from the contingent fact of the actual course of events; it thus allows of an ideal as conceivable in terms of what is actual.

Christianity, like Buddhism, preaches a doctrine of escape. It proclaims a doctrine whereby, through the treatment of evil, life is placed on a finer level. It overcomes evil with good. Buddhism makes itself probable by referring to its metaphysical theory. Christianity makes itself probable by referring to supreme religious moments in history.

Thus in respect to this crucial question of evil, Buddhism and Christianity are in en-

tirely different attitudes in respect to doctrine. Buddhism starts with the elucidatory
dogmas; Christianity starts with the elucidatory facts.

The problem of evil is only one among the
interests of rational religious thought. Another is the search after wisdom. In the Book
of Proverbs, in Ecclesiastes, and, among the
books of the Apocrypha, in the Wisdom of
Solomon, and in Ecclesiasticus, we find the
record of reflection upon general principles
embodied in proverbs, reflective, witty, and
homely.

The search after wisdom has its origin in
generalizations from experience:

> Two things have I required of thee; deny
> me them not before I die:
> Remove far from me vanity and lies: give
> me neither poverty nor riches; feed me with
> food convenient for me:
> Lest I be full, and deny thee, and say,
> Who is the Lord? or lest I be poor, and steal,
> and take the name of my God in vain!
>
> (Proverbs xxx. 7, 8, 9.)

The habit of reading the more exciting denunciations of the prophets is apt to conceal from us the amount of detached, middle-class common sense which also contributed to the religious tradition of the Jews. There is a keen appreciation of actual fact, even when the moral is not over-clear. For example:

> I returned, and saw under the sun, that the race is not to the swift, nor the battle to the strong, neither yet bread to the wise, nor yet riches to men of understanding, nor yet favour to men of skill; but time and chance happeneth to them all.
>
> (Ecclesiastes ix. 11.)

These two quotations express incontestable general truths, verified by the cynical wisdom of ages; and yet they are religion at a very low temperature. The point, thus illustrated, is that a rational religion must not confine itself to moments of emotional excitement. It must find its verification at all temperatures. It must admit the wisdom of the golden mean, in its season and for those whom it can claim by right of possession; and

it must admit "that time and chance hap-
peneth to them all."

The collection of Psalms is not properly a
reflective book. It is an expressive book. It
expresses the emotions natural to states of
mind hovering between a universal and a
tribal religious conception. There is joy in
the creative energy of a supreme ruler who is
also a tribal champion. There is the glorification of power, magnificent and barbaric:

> The earth is the Lord's, and the fulness
> thereof; the world, and they that dwell
> therein.
> Who is this King of glory? The Lord of
> hosts, he is the King of glory.
>
> (Psalms xxiv.)

Magnificent literature! But there is no solution here of the difficulties which haunted
Job. This worship of glory arising from
power is not only dangerous: it arises from
a barbaric conception of God. I suppose that
even the world itself could not contain the
bones of those slaughtered because of men
intoxicated by its attraction. This view of the

universe, in the guise of an Eastern empire ruled by a glorious tyrant, may have served its purpose. In its historical setting, it marks a religious ascent. The psalm quoted gives us its noblest expression. The other side comes out in the psalms expressing hate, psalms now generally withdrawn from public worship. The glorification of power has broken more hearts than it has healed.

Buddhism and Christianity find their origins respectively in two inspired moments of history: the life of the Buddha, and the life of Christ. The Buddha gave his doctrine to enlighten the world: Christ gave his life. It is for Christians to discern the doctrine. Perhaps in the end the most valuable part of the doctrine of the Buddha is its interpretation of his life.

We do not possess a systematic detailed record of the life of Christ; but we do possess a peculiarly vivid record of the first response to it in the minds of the first group of his disciples after the lapse of some years, with their recollections, interpretations, and incipient formularizations.

What we find depicted is a thoroughgoing

rationalization of the Jewish religion carried through with a boundless naïveté, and motived by a first-hand intuition into the nature of things.

The reported sayings of Christ are not formularized thought. They are descriptions of direct insight. The ideas are in his mind as immediate pictures, and not as analyzed in terms of abstract concepts. He sees intuitively the relations between good men and bad men; his expressions are not cast into the form of an analysis of the goodness and badness of man. His sayings are actions and not adjustments of concepts. He speaks in the lowest abstractions that language is capable of, if it is to be language at all and not the fact itself.

In the Sermon on the Mount, and in the Parables, there is no reasoning about the facts. They are seen with immeasurable innocence. Christ represents rationalism derived from direct intuition and divorced from dialectics.

The life of Christ is not an exhibition of over-ruling power. Its glory is for those who can discern it, and not for the world. Its power lies in its absence of force. It has the decisiveness of a supreme ideal, and that is why the history of the world divides at this point of time.

2. THE DESCRIPTION OF RELIGIOUS EXPERIENCE

The dogmas of religion are the attempts to formulate in precise terms the truths disclosed in the religious experience of mankind. In exactly the same way the dogmas of physical science are the attempts to formulate in precise terms the truths disclosed in the sense-perception of mankind.

In the previous section we have been considering religious experience in the concrete; we have now to define its general character. Some general descriptions of religion were given in the former lecture. It was stated that "Religion is force of belief cleansing the inward parts"; and again, that "Religion is the art and theory of the internal life of man, so far as it depends on the man himself, and on what is permanent in the nature of things": and again, "Religion is what the individual does with his own solitariness."

This point of the origin of rational religion in solitariness is fundamental. Religion is founded on the concurrence of three allied concepts in one moment of self-consciousness, concepts whose separate relationships to fact and whose mutual relations to each other are only to be settled jointly by some direct intuition into the ultimate character of the universe.

These concepts are:

1. That of the value of an individual for itself.
2. That of the value of the diverse individuals of the world for each other.
3. That of the value of the objective world which is a community derivative from the interrelations of its component individuals, and also necessary for the existence of each of these individuals.

The moment of religious consciousness starts from self-valuation, but it broadens into the concept of the world as a realm of adjusted values, mutually intensifying or mutually destructive. The intuition into the actual world gives a particular definite content to the bare notion of a principle determining the grading of values. It also exhibits emotions, purposes, and physical conditions, as subservient factors in the emergence of value.

In its solitariness the spirit asks, What, in the way of value, is the attainment of life? And it can find no such value till it has merged its individual claim with that of the objective universe. Religion is world-loyalty.

The spirit at once surrenders itself to this universal claim and appropriates it for itself. So far as it is dominated by religious experience, life is conditioned by this formative principle, equally individual and general, equally actual and beyond completed act, equally compelling recognition and permissive of disregard.

This principle is not a dogmatic formulation, but the intuition of immediate occasions as failing or succeeding in reference to the ideal relevant to them. There is a rightness attained or missed, with more or less completeness of attainment or omission.

This is a revelation of character, apprehended as we apprehend the characters of our friends. But in this case it is an apprehension of character permanently inherent in the nature of things.

There is a large concurrence in the negative doctrine that this religious experience does not include any direct intuition of a definite person, or individual. It is a character of permanent rightness, whose inherence in the nature of things modifies both efficient and final cause, so that the one conforms to harmonious conditions, and the other contrasts itself with an harmonious ideal. The harmony in the actual world is conformity with the character.

It is not true that every individual item of the universe conforms to this character in every detail. There will be some measure of conformity and some measure of diversity. The whole intuition of conformity and diversity forms the contrast which that item yields for the religious experience. So far as the conformity is incomplete, there is evil in the world.

The evidence for the assertion of general, though not universal, concurrence in the doctrine of no direct vision of a personal God, can only be found by a consideration of the religious thought in the civilized world. Here the sources of the evidence can only be indicated.

Throughout India and China religious thought, so far as it has been interpreted in precise form, disclaims the intuition of any ultimate personality substantial to the universe. This is true for Confucian philosophy, Buddhist philosophy, and Hindoo philosophy. There may be personal embodiments, but the substratum is impersonal.

Christian theology has also, in the main, adopted the position that there is no direct intuition of such an ultimate personal substratum for the world. It maintains the doctrine of the existence of a personal God as a truth, but holds that our belief in it is based upon inference. Most theologians hold that this inference is sufficiently obvious to be made by all men upon the basis of their individual personal experience. But, be this as it may, it is an inference and not a direct intuition. This is the general doctrine of those traditionalist churches which more especially claim the title of Catholic; and contrary doctrines have, I believe, been officially condemned by the Roman Catholic Church: for example, the religious philosophy of Rosmini.

Greek thought, when it began to scrutinize the traditional cults, took the same line. In some form or other all attempts to formulate the doctrines of a rational religion in ancient Greece took their stand upon the Pythagorean notion of a direct intuition of a righteousness in the nature of things, functioning as a condition, a critic, and an ideal. Divine personality was in the nature of an inference from the directly apprehended law of nature, so far as it *was* inferred. Of course, there were many cults of divine persons within the nature of things. The question in discussion concerns a divine person, substrate to the nature of things.

This question of the ultimate nature of direct religious experience is very fundamental to the religious situation of the modern world. In the first place, if you make religious experience to be the direct intuition of a personal being substrate to the universe, there is no widespread basis of agreement to appeal to. The main streams of religious thought start with direct contradictions to each other. For those who proceed in this way, and it is a usual form of modern appeal, there is only one hope—to supersede reason by emotion. Then you can prove anything, except to reasonable people. But reason is the safeguard of the objectivity of religion: it secures for it the general coherence denied to hysteria.

Another objection against this appeal to such an intuition, merely experienced in exceptional moments, is that the intuition is thereby a function of those moments. Anything which explains the origin of such moments, in respect to their emotional accompaniments, can then fairly be taken to be an explanation of the intuition. Thus the intuition becomes a private psychological habit, and is without general evidential force. This is the psychological interpretation which is fatal to evidence unable to maintain itself at all emotional temperatures amid great variety of environment.

Here a distinction must be drawn. Intuitions may first emerge as distinguished in consciousness under exceptional circumstances. But when some distinct idea has been once experienced, or suggested, it should then have its own independence of irrelevancies. Thus we may not know some arithmetical truth, and require some exceptional help to detect it. But when known, arithmetic is a permanent possession. The psychological interpretation, assigning a merely personal significance, holds when objective validity is claimed for an intuition which is only experienced in a set of discrete circumstances of definite specific character. The intuition may be clearer under such circumstances, but it should not be confined to them.

The wisdom of the main stream of Christian theology in refusing to countenance the notion of a direct vision of a personal God is manifest. For there is no consensus. The subordinate gods of the unrationalized religions —the religions of the heathen, as they are called—are not to the point; and when the great rationalized religions are examined, the majority lies the other way. As soon, however, as it comes to a question of rational interpretation, numbers rapidly sink in importance. Reason mocks at majorities.

But there is a large consensus, on the part of those who have rationalized their outlook, in favour of the concept of a rightness in things, partially conformed to and partially disregarded. So far as there is conscious determination of actions, the attainment of this conformity is an ultimate premise by reference to which our choice of immediate ends is criticised and swayed. The rational satisfaction or dissatisfaction in respect to any particular happening depends upon an intuition which is capable of being universalized. This universalization of what is discerned in a particular instance is the appeal to a general character inherent in the nature of things.

This intuition is not the discernment of a form of words, but of a type of character. It is characteristic of the learned mind to exalt words. Yet mothers can ponder many things in their hearts which their lips cannot express. These many things, which are thus known, constitute the ultimate religious evidence, beyond which there is no appeal.

3. GOD

To-day there is but one religious dogma in debate: What do you mean by "God"? And in this respect, to-day is like all its yesterdays. This is the fundamental religious dogma, and all other dogmas are subsidiary to it.

There are three main simple renderings of this concept before the world:

1. The Eastern Asiatic concept of an impersonal order to which the world conforms. This order is the self-ordering of the world; it is not the world obeying an imposed rule. The concept expresses the extreme doctrine of immanence.

2. The Semitic concept of a definite personal individual entity, whose existence is the one ultimate metaphysical fact, absolute and underivative, and who decreed and ordered the derivative existence which we call the actual world.

This Semitic concept is the rationalization of the tribal gods of the earlier communal religions. It expresses the extreme doctrine of transcendence.

3. The Pantheistic concept of an entity to be described in the terms of the Semitic concept, except that the actual world is a phase within the complete fact which is this ultimate individual entity. The actual world, conceived apart from God, is unreal. Its only reality is God's reality. The actual world has the reality of being a partial description of what God is. But in itself it is merely a certain mutuality of "appearance," which is a phase of the being of God. This is the extreme doctrine of monism.

It will be noticed that the Eastern Asiatic concept and the Pantheistic concept invert each other. According to the former concept, when we speak of God we are saying something about the world; and according to the latter concept, when we speak of the world we are saying something about God.

The Semitic concept and the Eastern Asiatic concept are directly opposed to each other, and any mediation between them must lead to complexity of thought. It is evident that the Semitic concept can very easily pass over into the Pantheistic concept. In fact, the history of philosophical theology in various Mahometan countries—Persia, for instance—shows that this passage has often been effected.

The main difficulties which the Semitic concept has to struggle with are two in number. One of them is that it leaves God completely outside metaphysical rationalization. We know, according to it, that He is such a being as to design and create this universe, and there our knowledge stops. If we mean by his goodness that He is the one self-existent, complete entity, then He is good. But such goodness must not be confused with the ordinary goodness of daily life. He is undeniably useful, because anything baffling can be ascribed to his direct decree.

The second difficulty of the concept is to get itself proved. The only possible proof would appear to be the "ontological proof" devised by Anselm, and revived by Descartes. According to this proof, the mere concept of such an entity allows us to infer its existence. Most philosophers and theologians reject this proof: for example, it is explicitly rejected by Cardinal Mercier in his *Manual of Scholastic Philosophy*.

Any proof which commences with the consideration of the character of the actual world cannot rise above the actuality of this world. It can only discover all the factors disclosed in the world as experienced. In other words, it may discover an immanent God, but not a God wholly transcendent. The difficulty can be put in this way: by considering the world we can find all the factors required by the total metaphysical situation; but we cannot discover anything not included in this totality of actual fact, and yet explanatory of it.

Christianity has not adopted any one of these clear alternatives. It has been true to its genius for keeping its metaphysics subordinate to the religious facts to which it appeals.

In the first place, it inherited the simple Semitic concept. All its founders naturally expressed themselves in those terms, and were addressing themselves to an audience who could only understand religion thus expressed.

But even here important qualifications have to be made. Christ himself introduces them. How far they were then new, or how far he is utilizing antecedent thoughts, is immaterial. The point is the decisive emphasis the notions receive in his teaching. The first point is the association of God with the Kingdom of Heaven, coupled with the explanation that "The Kingdom of Heaven is within you." The second point is the concept of God under the metaphor of a Father. The implications of this latter notion are expanded with moving insistence in the two Epistles by St. John, the author of the Gospel. To him we owe the phrase, "God is love."

Finally, in the Gospel of St. John, by the introduction of the doctrine of the Logos, a clear move is made towards the modification of the notion of the unequivocal personal unity of the Semitic God. Indeed, for most Christian Churches, the simple Semitic doctrine is now a heresy, both by reason of the modification of personal unity and also by the insistence on immanence.

The notion of immanence must be discriminated from that of omniscience. The Semitic God is omniscient; but, in addition to that, the Christian God is a factor in the universe. A few years ago a papyrus was found in an Egyptian tomb which proved to be an early Christian compilation called "The Sayings of Christ." Its exact authenticity and its exact authority do not concern us. I am quoting it as evidence of the mentality of many Christians in Egypt during the first few Christian centuries. At that date Egypt supplied the theological leaders of Christian thought. We find in these Logia of Christ the saying, "Cleave the wood, and I am there." This is merely one example of an emphatic assertion of immanence, and shows a serious divergence from the Semitic concept.

Immanence is a well-known modern doctrine. The points to be noticed are that it is implicit in various parts of the New Testament, and was explicit in the first theological epoch of Christianity. Christian theology was then Platonic; it followed John rather than Paul.

4. THE QUEST OF GOD

The modern world has lost God and is seeking him. The reason for the loss stretches far back in the history of Christianity. In respect to its doctrine of God the Church gradually returned to the Semitic concept, with the addition of the threefold personality. It is a concept which is clear, terrifying, and unprovable. It was supported by an unquestioned religious tradition. It was also supported by the conservative instinct of society, and by a history and a metaphysic both constructed expressly for that purpose. Moreover, to dissent was death.

On the whole, the Gospel of love was turned into a Gospel of fear. The Christian world was composed of terrified populations.

"The fear of the Lord is the beginning of knowledge," said the Proverb (i. 7). Yet this is an odd saying, if it be true that "God is love."

In flaming fire taking vengeance on them that know not God, and that obey not the gospel of our Lord Jesus Christ; says Paul.
Who shall be punished with everlasting destruction from the presence of the Lord, and from the glory of his power.
(II Thessalonians i. 8, 9.)

The populations did well to be terrified at such ambiguous good tidings, which lost no emphasis in their promulgation.

If the modern world is to find God, it must find him through love and not through fear, with the help of John and not of Paul. Such a conclusion is true and represents a common-place of modern thought. But it is only a very superficial rendering of the facts.

As a rebound from dogmatic intolerance, the simplicity of religious truth has been a favorite axiom of liberalizing theologians. It is difficult to understand upon what evidence this notion is based. In the physical world as science advances, we discern a complexity of interrelations. There is a certain simplicity of dominant ideas, but modern physics does not disclose a simple world.

To reduce religion to a few simple notions seems an arbitrary solution of the problem before us. It may be common sense; but is it true? In view of the horrors produced by bigotry, it is natural for sensitive thinkers to minimize religious dogmas. But such pragmatic reasons are dangerous guides.

This procedure ends by basing religion on those few ideas which in the circumstances of the time are most effective in producing pleasing emotions and agreeable conduct. If our trust is in the ultimate power of reason as a discipline for the discernment of truth, we have no right to impose such *a priori* conditions. All simplifications of religious dogma are shipwrecked upon the rock of the problem of evil.

As a particular application, we may believe that the various doctrines about God have not suffered chiefly from their complexity. They have represented extremes of simplicity, so far as they have been formulated for the great rationalistic religions. The three extremes of simple notions should not represent in our eyes mutually exclusive concepts, from among which we are to choose one and reject the others.

It cannot be true that contradictory notions can apply to the same fact. Thus reconcilement of these contrary concepts must be sought in a more searching analysis of the meaning of the terms in which they are phrased.

The man who refused to admit that two and two make four, until he knew what use was to be made of this premise, had some justification. At a certain abstract level of thought, such statements are absolutely true. But once you desert that level, you admit fundamental transformations of meaning. Language cloaks the most profound ideas under its simplest words. For example, in "two and two make four," the words "and" and "make" entirely depend for their meaning upon the application which you are giving to the statement.

Analogously, in expressing our conception of God, words such as "personal" and "impersonal," "entity," "individuality," "actual," require the closest careful watching, lest in different connections we should use them in different senses, not to speak of the danger of failing to use them in any determinate sense.

But it is impossible to fix the sense of fundamental terms except by reference to some definite metaphysical way of conceiving the most penetrating description of the universe.

Thus rational religion must have recourse to metaphysics for a scrutiny of its terms. At the same time it contributes its own independent evidence, which metaphysics must take account of in framing its description.

This mutual dependence is illustrated in all topics. For example, I have mentioned above that in modern Europe history and metaphysics have been constructed with the purpose of supporting the Semitic concept of God. To some extent this is justifiable, because both history and metaphysics must presuppose some canons by which to guide themselves.

The result is that you cannot confine any important reorganization to one sphere of thought alone. You cannot shelter theology from science, or science from theology; nor can you shelter either of them from metaphysics, or metaphysics from either of them. There is no short cut to truth.

Religion, therefore, while in the framing of dogmas it must admit modifications from the complete circle of our knowledge, still brings its own contribution of immediate experience.

That contribution is in the first place the recognition that our existence is more than a succession of bare facts. We live in a common world of mutual adjustment, of intelligible relations, of valuations, of zest after purposes, of joy and grief, of interest concentrated on self, of interest directed beyond self, of short-time and long-time failures or successes, of different layers of feeling, of life-weariness and of life-zest.

There is a quality of life which lies always beyond the mere fact of life; and when we include the quality in the fact, there is still omitted the quality of the quality. It is not true that the finer quality is the direct associate of obvious happiness or obvious pleasure. Religion is the direct apprehension that, beyond such happiness and such pleasure, there remains the function of what is actual and passing, that it contributes its quality as an immortal fact to the order which informs the world.

III: BODY AND SPIRIT

I. RELIGION AND METAPHYSICS

Religion requires a metaphysical backing; for its authority is endangered by the intensity of the emotions which it generates. Such emotions are evidence of some vivid experience; but they are a very poor guarantee for its correct interpretation.

Thus dispassionate criticism of religious belief is beyond all things necessary. The foundations of dogma must be laid in a rational metaphysics which criticises meanings, and endeavours to express the most general concepts adequate for the all-inclusive universe.

This position has never been seriously doubted, though in practice it is often evaded. One of the most serious periods of neglect occurred in the middle of the nineteenth century, through the dominance of the historical interest.

It is a curious delusion that the rock upon which our beliefs can be founded is an historical investigation. You can only interpret the past in terms of the present. The present is all that you have; and unless in this present you can find general principles which interpret the present as including a representation of the whole community of existents, you cannot move a step beyond your little patch of immediacy.

Thus history presupposes a metaphysic. It can be objected that we believe in the past and talk about it without settling our metaphysical principles. That is certainly the case. But you can only deduce metaphysical dogmas from your interpretation of the past on the basis of a prior metaphysical interpretation of the present.*

In so far as your metaphysical beliefs are implicit, you vaguely interpret the past on the

* By "metaphysics" I mean the science which seeks to discover the general ideas which are indispensably relevant to the analysis of everything that happens.

lines of the present. But when it comes to the primary metaphysical data, the world of which you are immediately conscious is the whole datum.

This criticism applies equally to a science or to a religion which hopes to justify itself without any appeal to metaphysics. The difference is that religion is the longing of the spirit that the facts of existence should find their justification in the nature of existence. "My soul thirsteth for God," writes the Psalmist.

But science can leave its metaphysics implicit and retire behind our belief in the pragmatic value of its general descriptions. If religion does that, it admits that its dogmas are merely pleasing ideas for the purpose of stimulating its emotions. Science (at least as a temporary methodological device) can rest upon a naïve faith; religion is the longing for justification. When religion ceases to seek for penetration, for clarity, it is sinking back into its lower forms. The ages of faith are the ages of rationalism.

2. THE CONTRIBUTION OF RELIGION
TO METAPHYSICS

In the previous lectures religious experience was considered as a fact. It consists of a certain widespread, direct apprehension of a character exemplified in the actual universe. Such a character includes in itself certain metaphysical presuppositions. In so far as we trust the objectivity of the religious intuitions, to that extent we must also hold that the metaphysical doctrines are well founded.

It is for this reason that in the previous lecture the broadest view of religious experience was insisted on. If, at this stage of thought, we include points of radical divergence between the main streams, the whole evidential force is indefinitely weakened. Thus religious experience cannot be taken as contributing to metaphysics any direct evidence for a personal God in any sense transcendent or creative.

The universe, thus disclosed, is through and through interdependent. The body pollutes the mind, the mind pollutes the body. Physical energy sublimates itself into zeal; conversely, zeal stimulates the body. The biological ends pass into ideals of standards, and the formation of standards affects the biological facts. The individual is formative of the society, the society is formative of the individual. Particular evils infect the whole world, particular goods point the way of escape.

The world is at once a passing shadow and a final fact. The shadow is passing into the fact, so as to be constitutive of it; and yet the fact is prior to the shadow. There is a kingdom of heaven prior to the actual passage of actual things, and there is the same kingdom finding its completion through the accomplishment of this passage.

But just as the kingdom of heaven transcends the natural world, so does this world transcend the kingdom of heaven. For the world is evil, and the kingdom is good. The kingdom is in the world, and yet not of the world.

The actual world, the world of experiencing, and of thinking, and of physical activity, is a community of many diverse entities; and these entities contribute to, or derogate from, the common value of the total community. At the same time, these actual entities are, for themselves, their own value, individual and separable. They add to the common stock and yet they suffer alone. The world is a scene of solitariness in community.

The individuality of entities is just as important as their community. The topic of religion is individuality in community.

3. A METAPHYSICAL DESCRIPTION

A metaphysics is a description. Its discussion so as to elucidate its accuracy is necessary, but it is foreign to the description. The tests of accuracy are logical coherence, adequacy, and exemplification. A metaphysical description takes its origin from one select field of interest. It receives its confirmation by establishing itself as adequate and as exemplified in other fields of interest.* The following description is set out for immediate comparison with the deliverances of religious experience.

There are many ways of analyzing the universe, conceived as that which is comprehensive of all that there is. In a description it is thus necessary to correlate these different routes of analysis. First, consider the analysis into (1) the actual world, passing in time; and (2) those elements which go to its formation.

Such formative elements are not themselves actual and passing; they are the factors which are either non-actual or non-temporal, disclosed in the analysis of what is both actual and temporal.

They constitute the formative character of the actual temporal world. We know nothing beyond this temporal world and the formative elements which jointly constitute its character. The temporal world and its formative elements constitute for us the all-inclusive universe.

* For the application to science of this description, cf. my *Science and the Modern World*.

These formative elements are:

1. The creativity whereby the actual world has its character of temporal passage to novelty.

2. The realm of ideal entities, or forms, which are in themselves not actual, but are such that they are exemplified in everything that is actual, according to some proportion of relevance.

3. The actual but non-temporal entity whereby the indetermination of mere creativity is transmuted into a determinate freedom. This non-temporal actual entity is what men call God—the supreme God of rationalized religion.

A further elucidation of the status of these formative elements is only to be obtained by having recourse to another mode of analysis of the actual world.

The actual temporal world can be analyzed into a multiplicity of occasions of actualization. These are the primary actual units of which the temporal world is composed. Call

each such occasion an "epochal occasion."
Then the actual world is a community of
epochal occasions. In the physical world each
epochal occasion is a definite limited physical
event, limited both as to space and time, but
with time-duration as well as with its full
spatial dimensions.

The epochal occasions are the primary
units of the actual community, and the community is composed of the units. But each
unit has in its nature a reference to every
other member of the community, so that each
unit is a microcosm representing in itself the
entire all-inclusive universe.

These epochal occasions are the creatures.
The reason for the temporal character of the
actual world can now be given by reference
to the creativity and the creatures. For the
creativity is not separable from its creatures.
Thus the creatures remain with the creativity.
Accordingly, the creativity for a creature becomes the creativity with the creature, and
thereby passes into another phase of itself.
It is now the creativity for a new creature.
Thus there is a transition of the creative ac-

tion, and this transition exhibits itself, in the physical world, in the guise of routes of temporal succession.

This protean character of the creativity forbids us from conceiving it as an actual entity. For its character lacks determinateness. It equally prevents us from considering the temporal world as a definite actual creature. For the temporal world is an essential incompleteness. It has not the character of a definite matter of fact, such as attaches to an event in past history, viewed from a present standpoint.

An epochal occasion is a concretion. It is a mode in which diverse elements come together into a real unity. Apart from that concretion, these elements stand in mutual isolation. Thus an actual entity is the outcome of a creative synthesis, individual and passing.

The various elements which are thus brought into unity are the other creatures and the ideal forms and God. These elements are not a mere unqualified aggregate. In such a case there could only be one creature. In the concretion the creatures are qualified by the ideal forms, and conversely the ideal forms are qualified by the creatures. Thus the epochal occasion, which is thus emergent, has in its own nature the other creatures under the aspect of these forms, and analogously it includes the forms under the aspect of these creatures. It is thus a definite limited creature, emergent in consequence of the limitations thus mutually imposed on each other by the elements.

4. GOD AND THE MORAL ORDER

The inclusion of God in every creature shows itself in the determination whereby a definite result is emergent. God is that non-temporal actuality which has to be taken account of in every creative phase. Any such phase is determinate having regard to its antecedents, and in this determination exhibits conformity to a common order.

The boundless wealth of possibility in the realm of abstract form would leave each creative phase still indeterminate, unable to synthesize under determinate conditions the creatures from which it springs. The definite determination which imposes ordered balance on the world requires an actual entity imposing its own unchanged consistency of character on every phase.

Thus creative indetermination attains its measure of determination. A simpler metaphysic would result if we could stop at this conclusion. A complete determinism would thus mean the complete self-consistency of the temporal world. This is the conclusion of all thinkers who are inclined to trust to the adequacy of metaphysical concepts.

The difficulty of this conclusion comes when we confront the theory with the facts of the world. If the theory of complete determinism, by reason of the necessity of conformation with the nature of God, holds true, then the evil in the world is in conformity with the nature of God.

Now evil is exhibited in physical suffering, mental suffering, and loss of the higher experience in favour of the lower experience. The common character of all evil is that its realization in fact involves that there is some concurrent realization of a purpose towards elimination. The purpose is to secure the avoidance of evil. The fact of the instability of evil is the moral order in the world.

Evil, triumphant in its enjoyment, is so far good in itself; but beyond itself it is evil in its character of a destructive agent among things greater than itself. In the summation of the more complete fact it has secured a descent towards nothingness, in contrast to the creativeness of what can without qualification be termed good. Evil is positive and destructive; what is good is positive and creative.

This instability of evil does not necessarily lead to progress. On the contrary, the evil in itself leads to the world losing forms of attainment in which that evil manifests itself. Either the species ceases to exist, or it sinks back into a stage in which it ranks below the possibility of that form of evil. For example, a species whose members are always in pain will either cease to exist, or lose the delicacy of perception which results in that pain, or develop a finer and more subtle relationship among its bodily parts.

Thus evil promotes its own elimination by destruction, or degradation, or by elevation. But in its own nature it is unstable. It must be noted that the state of degradation to which evil leads, when accomplished, is not in itself evil, except by comparison with what might have been. A hog is not an evil beast, but when a man is degraded to the level of a hog, with the accompanying atrophy of finer elements, he is no more evil than a hog. The evil of the final degradation lies in the comparison of what is with what might have been. During the process of degradation the comparison is an evil for the man himself, and at its final stage it remains an evil for others.

But in this last point respecting the evil for others, it becomes plain that, with a sufficiently comprehensive view, a stable state of final degradation is not reached. For the relationships with society and the indirect effects have to be taken into account. Also destruction when accomplished is not an evil for the thing destroyed. For there is no such thing. Again the evil lies in the loss to the social environment. There is evil when things are at cross purposes.

The contrast in the world between evil and good is the contrast between the turbulence of evil and the "peace which passeth all understanding." There is a self-preservation inherent in that which is good in itself. Its destruction may come from without but not from within. Good people of narrow sympathies are apt to be unfeeling and unprogressive, enjoying their egotistical goodness. Their case, on a higher level, is analogous to that of the man completely degraded to a hog. They have reached a state of stable goodness, so far as their own interior life is concerned. This type of moral correctitude is, on a larger view, so like evil that the distinction is trivial.

Thus if God be an actual entity which enters into every creative phase and yet is above change, He must be exempt from internal inconsistency which is the note of evil. Since God is actual, He must include in himself a synthesis of the total universe. There is, therefore, in God's nature the aspect of the realm of forms as qualified by the world, and the aspect of the world as qualified by the forms. His completion, so that He is exempt from transition into something else, must mean that his nature remains self-consistent in relation to all change.

Thus God is the measure of the aesthetic consistency of the world. There is some consistency in creative action, because it is conditioned by his immanence.

If we trace the evil in the world to the determinism derived from God, then the inconsistency in the world is derived from the consistency of God. Also the incompletion in the world is derivative from the completion of God.

The temporal world exhibits two sides of itself. On one side it exhibits an order in matter of fact, and a self-contrast with ideals, which show that its creative passage is subject to the immanence of an unchanging actual entity. On the other side its incompletion, and its evil, show that the temporal world is to be construed in terms of additional formative elements which are not definable in the terms which are applicable to God.

5. VALUE AND THE PURPOSE OF GOD

The purpose of God is the attainment of value in the temporal world. An active purpose is the adjustment of the present for the sake of adjustment of value in the future, immediately or remotely.

Value is inherent in actuality itself. To be an actual entity is to have a self-interest. This self-interest is a feeling of self-valuation; it is an emotional tone. The value of other things, not one's self, is the derivative value of being elements contributing to this ultimate self-interest. This self-interest is the interest of what one's existence, as in that epochal occasion, comes to. It is the ultimate enjoyment of being actual.

But the actuality is the enjoyment, and this enjoyment is the experiencing of value. For an epochal occasion is a microcosm inclusive of the whole universe. This unification of the universe, whereby its various elements are combined into aspects of each other, is an atomic unit within the real world.

Such an ultimate concrete fact is of the nature of an act of perceptivity. But, if we are speaking of the non-mental facts, such perceptivity is blind. It is without reflective consciousness; it is the self-value of its own microcosmic apprehension. The self-value is the unit fact which emerges. In calling it a perceptivity, or an apprehension, we are already analyzing it into the separate ingredients which go to form the one emergent thing. Each actual entity is an arrangement of the whole universe, actual and ideal, whereby there is constituted that self-value which is the entity itself.

Thus the epochal occasion has two sides. On one side it is a mode of creativity bringing together the universe. This side is the occasion as the cause of itself, its own creative act. We are here conceiving the creation as the reverse of our analysis. For in our description we are holding the elements apart; whereas in the creation they are put together.

On the other side, the occasion is the creature. This creature is that one emergent fact.

This fact is the self-value of the creative act. But there are not two actual entities, the creativity and the creature. There is only one entity which is the self-creating creature.

The description of the variety of aspects, under which the various actual occasions enter into each other's natures, is the description of the various relationships within the real physical and spiritual worlds.

The mental occasion is derivative from its physical counterpart. It is also equally of the character of a perceptivity issuing into value-feeling, but it is a reflective perceptivity.

There are two routes of creative passage from a physical occasion. One is towards another physical occasion, and the other is towards the derivative reflective occasion. The physical route links together physical occasions as successive temporal incidents in the life of a body. The other route links this bodily life with a correlative mental life. A mental occasion is an ultimate fact in the spiritual world, just as a physical occasion of blind perceptivity is an ultimate fact in the physical world. There is an essential reference from one world to the other.

There is no such thing as bare value. There is always a specific value, which is the created unit of feeling arising out of the specific mode of concretion of the diverse elements. These different specific value-feelings are comparable amid their differences; and the ground for this comparability is what is here termed "value."

This comparability grades the various occasions in respect to the intensiveness of value. The zero of intensiveness means the collapse of actuality. All intensive quantity is merely the contribution of some one element in the synthesis to this one intensiveness of value.

Various occasions are thus comparable in respect to their relative depths of actuality. Occasions differ in importance of actuality. Thus the purpose of God in the attainment of value is in a sense a creative purpose. Apart from God, the remaining formative elements would fail in their functions. There would be no creatures, since, apart from harmonious order, the perceptive fusion would be a confusion neutralizing achieved feeling. Here "feeling" is used as a synonym for "actuality."

The adjustment is the reason for the world. It is not the case that there is an actual world which accidentally happens to exhibit an order of nature. There is an actual world because there is an order in nature. If there were no order, there would be no world. Also since there is a world, we know that there is an order. The ordering entity is a necessary element in the metaphysical situation presented by the actual world.

This line of thought extends Kant's argument. He saw the necessity for God in the moral order. But with his metaphysics he rejected the argument from the cosmos. The metaphysical doctrine, here expounded, finds the foundations of the world in the aesthetic experience, rather than—as with Kant—in the cognitive and conceptive experience. All order is therefore aesthetic order, and the moral order is merely certain aspects of aesthetic order. The actual world is the outcome of the aesthetic order, and the aesthetic order is derived from the immanence of God.

6. BODY AND MIND

Descartes grounded his philosophy on an entirely different metaphysical description of the actual world. He started with cogitating minds, and with extended bodies which are the organic and inorganic bits of matter.

Now in some sense no one doubts but that there are bodies and minds. The only point at issue is the status of such bodies and minds in the scheme of things. Descartes affirmed that they were individual substances, so that each bit of matter is a substance, and each mind is a substance. He also states what he means by a substance. He says:

And when we conceive of substance, we merely conceive an existent thing which requires nothing but itself in order to exist. To speak truth, nothing but God answers to this description as being that which is absolutely self-sustaining, for we perceive that there is no other created thing which can exist without being sustained by his power. . . .

Created substances, however, whether corporeal or thinking, may be conceived under this common concept; for they are things which need only the concurrence of God in order to exist. . . . When we perceive any attribute, we therefore conclude that some existing thing or substance to which it may be attributed, is necessarily present.*

These sentences are a summary of the presupposition of scientific thought in recent centuries: that the world is composed of bits of stuff with attributes. There are insuperable difficulties in Descartes' view which have led to attempts at simplification, keeping his general supposition of stuff with attributes.

Note that Descartes presupposes three types of substance—namely, God, bits of matter, minds. Descartes' proof of the existence of God is accepted by very few philosophers, religious or otherwise. Indeed, given his starting point, it is difficult to see how any proof can be found.

* *Principles of Philosophy*, LI and LII. Translated by Haldane and Ross.

The simplifications all concern dropping either one or two of these types of substances. For example, dropping God, and retaining only matter and mind; or dropping God and minds, and retaining the matter, as with Hobbes; or dropping matter, and retaining God and minds, as with Berkeley; or dropping matter and minds, and retaining God alone. In this latter case, the temporal world becomes an appearance forming an attribute of God.

But the main point of all such philosophies is that they presuppose individual substance, either one or many individual substances, "which requires nothing but itself in order to exist." This presupposition is exactly what is denied in the more Platonic description which has been given in this lecture. There is no entity, not even God, "which requires nothing but itself in order to exist."

According to the doctrine of this lecture, every entity is in its essence social and requires the society in order to exist. In fact, the society for each entity, actual or ideal, is the all inclusive universe, including its ideal forms.

But Descartes has the great merit that he states facts which any philosophy must fit into its scheme. There *are* bits of matter, and there *are* minds. Both matter and mind have to be fitted into the metaphysical scheme.

Now, according to the doctrine of this lecture, the most individual actual entity is a definite act of perceptivity. So matter and mind, which persist through a route of such occasions, must be relatively abstract; and they must gain their specific individualities from their respective routes. The character of a bit of matter must be something common to each occasion of its route; and analogously, the character of a mind must be something common to each occasion of its route. Each bit of matter, and each mind, is a subordinate community—in that sense analogously to the actual world.

But each occasion, in its character of being a finished creature, is a value of some definite specific sort. Thus a mind must be a route whose various occasions exhibit some community of type of value. Similarly a bit of matter—or an electron—must be a route whose various occasions exhibit some community of type of value.

Again in such a route—material or mental —the environment will also partially determine the forms of the occasions. But that which the occasions have in common, so as to form a route of mind or a route of matter, must be derived by inheritance from the antecedent members of the route. The environment may favour this inheritance or may obstruct it. But such influence must be in the background so that there is a real transmission of the common element along the route.

In the case of men and animals, there are obviously routes of mind and routes of matter in the very closest connection, which we will consider more particularly in a moment. In the case of a bit of inorganic matter, any associate route of mentality seems to be negligible.

A belief in purely spiritual beings means, on this metaphysical theory, that there are routes of mentality in respect to which associate material routes are negligible, or entirely absent. At the present moment the orthodox belief is that for all men after death there are such routes, and that for all animals after death there are no such routes.

Also at present it is generally held that a purely spiritual being is necessarily immortal. The doctrine here developed gives no warrant for such a belief. It is entirely neutral on the question of immortality, or on the existence of purely spiritual beings other than God. There is no reason why such a question should not be decided on more special evidence, religious or otherwise, provided that it is trustworthy. In this lecture we are merely considering evidence with a certain breadth of extension throughout mankind. Until that evidence has yielded its systematic theory, special evidence is indefinitely weakened in its effect.

7. THE CREATIVE PROCESS

This account of what is meant by the enduring existence of matter and of mind explains such endurance as exemplifying the order immanent in the world. The solid earth survives because there is an order laid upon the creativity in virtue of which second after second, minute after minute, hour after hour, day after day, year after year, century after century, age after age, the creative energy finds in the maintenance of that complex form a centre of experienced perceptivity focusing the universe into one unity.

It survives because the universe is a process of attaining instances of definite experience out of its own elements. Each such instance embraces the whole, omitting nothing, whether it be ideal form or actual fact. But it brings them into its own unity of feeling under gradations of relevance and of irrelevance, and thereby by this limitation issues into that definite experience which it is.

Accordingly, any given instance of experience is only possible so far as the antecedent facts permit. For they are required in order to constitute it. The maintenance, throughout ages of life history, of a given type of experience, in instance after instance of its separate occasions, requires, therefore, the stable order of the actual world.

The creative process is thus to be discerned in that transition by which one occasion, already actual, enters into the birth of another instance of experienced value. There is not one simple line of transition from occasion to occasion, though there may be a dominant line. The whole world conspires to produce a new creation. It presents to the creative process its opportunities and its limitations.

The limitations are the opportunities. The essence of depth of actuality—that is of vivid experience—is definiteness. Now to be definite always means that all the elements of a complex whole contribute to some *one* effect, to the exclusion of others. The creative process is a process of exclusion to the same extent as it is a process of inclusion. In this connection "to exclude" means to relegate to irrelevance in the aesthetic unity, and "to include" means to elicit relevance to that unity.

The birth of a new instance is the passage into novelty. Consider how any one actual fact, which I will call the *ground*, can enter into the creative process. The novelty which enters into the derivate instance is the information of the actual world with a new set of ideal forms. In the most literal sense the lapse of time is the renovation of the world with ideas. A great philosopher* has said that time is the mind of space. In respect to one particular new birth of one centre of experience, this novelty of ideal forms will be called the "consequent." Thus we are now considering the particular relevance of the consequent to the particular ground supplied by one antecedent occasion.

The derivate includes the fusion of the particular ground with the consequent, so far as the consequent is graded by its relevance to that ground.

In this fusion of ground with consequent, the creative process brings together something which is actual and something which, at its entry into that process, is not actual. The process is the achievement of actuality by the ideal consequent, in virtue of its union with the actual ground. In the phrase of Aristotle, the process is the fusion of being with not-being.

* Cf. Alexander, *Mind, Space, and Deity*, Vol. II, p. 43, *et passim.*

The birth of a new aesthetic experience depends on the maintenance of two principles by the creative purpose:

　　1. The novel consequent must be graded in relevance so as to preserve some identity of character with the ground.

　　2. The novel consequent must be graded in relevance so as to preserve some contrast with the ground in respect to that same identity of character.

These two principles are derived from the doctrine that an actual fact is a fact of aesthetic experience. All aesthetic experience is feeling arising out of the realization of contrast under identity.

Thus the consequent must agree with the ground in general type so as to preserve definiteness, but it must contrast with it in respect to contrary instances so as to obtain vividness and quality. In the physical world, this principle of contrast under an identity expresses itself in the physical law that vibration enters into the ultimate nature of atomic organisms. Vibration is the recurrence of contrast within identity of type. The whole possibility of measurement in the physical world depends on this principle. To measure is to count vibrations.

Thus physical quantities are aggregates of physical vibrations, and physical vibrations are the expression among the abstractions of physical science of the fundamental principle of aesthetic experience.

Another example of this same principle is to be found in the connection between body and mind. Both mind and body refer to their life-history of separate concrete occasions. So the connection which we seek is to be found in the creative process relating a physical occasion, in the life of the body, to its corresponding mental occasion in the life of the mind.

The physical occasion enters into the mental occasion, as already actual, and as contributing to its ground. The reversion from its ground, which the consequent of ideal novelty must exhibit, is now of the most fundamental character. The reversion is the undoing of the synthesis exhibited in the ground. Thus the transition from bodily occasion to mental occasion exhibits a new dimension of transition from that exhibited in the transition from bodily occasion to bodily occasion. In the latter transition there is the novelty of contrast within the one concept of synthesis. In the former, the contrast is the contrast of synthesis itself with its opposite, which is analysis.

Thus in the birth of the mental occasion the consequent of ideal novelty enters into reality, and possesses an analytic force over against the synthetic ground. Ideal forms thus synthesized into a mental occasion are termed concepts. Concepts meet blind experience with an analytic force. Their synthesis with physical occasion, as ground, is the perceptive analysis of the blind physical occasion in respect to its degree of relevance to the concepts.

The phrase "immediate experience" can have either of two meanings, according as it refers to the physical or to the mental occasion. It may mean a complete concretion of physical relationships in the unity of a blind perceptivity. In this sense "immediate experience" means an ultimate physical fact.

But in a secondary, and more usual, sense it means the consciousness of physical experience. Such consciousness is a mental occasion. It has the character of being an analysis of physical experience by synthesis with the concepts involved in the mentality. Such analysis is incomplete, because it is dependent on the limitations of the concepts. This limition arises from the grading of the relevance of the concepts in the mental occasion. The most complete concrete fact is dipolar, physical and mental. But, for some specific purpose, the proportion of importance, as shared between the two poles, may vary from negligibility to dominance of either pole.

The value realized in the mental occasion is knowledge-value. This knowledge-value is the issue of the full character of the creativity into the creature world. There is nothing in the creativity which fails to issue into the actual world. Thus the creativity with a purpose issues into the mental creature conscious of an ideal. Also God, as conditioning the creativity with his harmony of apprehension, issues into the mental creature as moral judgment according to a perfection of ideals.

The order of the world is no accident. There is nothing actual which could be actual without some measure of order. The religious insight is the grasp of this truth: That the order of the world, the depth of reality of the world, the value of the world in its whole and in its parts, the beauty of the world, the zest of life, the peace of life, and the mastery of evil, are all bound together— not accidentally, but by reason of this truth: that the universe exhibits a creativity with infinite freedom, and a realm of forms with infinite possibilities; but that this creativity and these forms are together impotent to achieve actuality apart from the completed ideal harmony, which is God.

IV: TRUTH AND CRITICISM

I. THE DEVELOPMENT OF DOGMA

In human nature there is no such separate function as a special religious sense. In making this assertion, I am agreeing with the following quotation:

> Those who tend to identify religious experience with the activity of some peculiar organ or element of the mental life have recently made much of the subconscious. Here there seems to be a safe retreat for the hard-pressed advocates of the uniqueness of religious experience.*

*Cf. Prof. E. S. Ames, *The Psychology of Religious Experience*, p. 291.

Religious truth must be developed from knowledge acquired when our ordinary senses and intellectual operations are at their highest pitch of discipline. To move one step from this position towards the dark recesses of abnormal psychology is to surrender finally any hope of a solid foundation for religious doctrine.

Religion starts from the generalization of final truths first perceived as exemplified in particular instances. These truths are amplified into a coherent system and applied to the interpretation of life. They stand or fall —like other truths—by their success in this interpretation. The peculiar character of religious truth is that it explicitly deals with values. It brings into our consciousness that permanent side of the universe which we can care for. It thereby provides a meaning, in terms of value, for our own existence, a meaning which flows from the nature of things.

It is not true, however, that we observe best when we are entirely devoid of emotion. Unless there is a direction of interest, we do not observe at all. Further, our capacity for observation is limited. Accordingly, when we are observing some things, we are in a bad position for observing other things.

Thus there are certain emotional states which are most favourable for a peculiar concentration on topics of religious interest, just as other states facilitate the apprehension of arithmetical truths. Also, emotional states are related to states of the body. Most people are more likely to make arithmetical slips when they are tired in the evening. But we still believe that arithmetic holds good from sundown to cockcrow.

Again, it is not true that all people are on a level in respect to their perceptive powers. Some people appear to realize continuously, and at a higher level, types of emotional and perceptive experience, which we recognize as corresponding to those periods of our own lives most worthy of confidence for that sort of experience. In so far as what they say interprets our own best moments, it is reasonable to trust to the evidential force of their experience.

These considerations are all commonplaces, but it is necessary to keep them clearly in mind when we endeavour to form our philosophy of religious knowledge.

A dogma is the precise enunciation of a general truth, divested so far as possible from particular exemplification. Such precise expression is in the long run a condition for vivid realization, for effectiveness, for apprehension of width of scope, and for survival.

For example, when the Greeks, such as Pythagoras or Euclid, formulated accurately mathematical dogmas, the general truths which the Egyptians had acted upon for more than thirty generations became thereby of greater importance.

It is not the case, however, that our apprehension of a general truth is dependent upon its accurate verbal expression. For it would follow that we could never be dissatisfied with the verbal expression of something that we had never apprehended. But this consciousness of failure to express our accurate meaning must have haunted most of us.

For example, the notion of irrational number had been used in mathematics for over two thousand years before it received accurate definition in the last quarter of the nineteenth century. Also, Newton and Leibnitz introduced the differential calculus, which was the foundation of modern mathematical physics. But the mathematical notions involved did not receive adequate verbal expression for two hundred and fifty years.

Such recondite examples are quite unnecessary. We know more of the characters of those who are dear to us than we can express accurately in words. We may recognize the truth of some statement about them. It will be a new statement about something which we had already apprehended but had never formulated.

This example brings out another fact: that a one-sided formulation may be true, but may have the effect of a lie by its distortion of emphasis. Such distortion does not stand in its character of a truth, but depends upon those who are affected by it. So far as the make-up of an individual mind is concerned, there is a proportion in truth as well as in art.

Thus an ill-balanced zeal for the propagation of dogma bears witness to a certain coarseness of aesthetic sensitiveness. It shows a strain of indifference—due perhaps to arrogance, perhaps to rashness, perhaps to mere ignorance—a strain of indifference to the fact that others may require a proportion of formulation different from that suitable for ourselves. Perhaps our pet dogmas require correction: they may even be wrong.

The fate of a word has to the historian the value of a document. The modern unfavourable implications of the kindred words, dogma, dogmatic, dogmatist, tell the story of some failure in habits of thought. The word "dogma" originally means an "opinion," and thence more especially a "philosophic opinion." Thus, for example, the Greek physician, Galen, uses the phrase "dogmatic physicians" to mean "physicians who guide themselves by general principles"—surely a praiseworthy practice. The nearest Greek Dictionary will give this elementary information. But the dictionary—and this is why I have quoted it—gives an ominous addition to the information about Galen. It says that Galen contrasts "dogmatic physicians" with "empiric physicians." If you then refer to the word "empiric," you will find that "empiric physicians" contended that "experience was the one thing needful." In this lecture we have to investigate the application to religion of this contrast between "dogmatic" and "empiric."

The philosophy of expression is only now receiving its proper attention.[*] In the framing of dogmas it is only possible to use ideas which have received a distinct, well-recognized signification. Also, no idea is determinate in a vacuum: It has its being as one of a system of ideas. A dogma is the expression of a fact as it appears within a certain sphere of thought. You cannot convey a dogma by merely translating the words; you must also understand the system of thought to which it is relevant. To take a very obvious example, "The Fatherhood of God" is a phrase which would have a significance for a Roman citizen of the early Republic different from that which it has for a modern American— stern for the one, tender for the other.

In estimating the validity of a dogma, it must be projected against the alternatives to

[*] Cf. *Symbolism and Truth*, by R. M. Eaton. Harvard University Press, 1925.

it within that sphere of thought. You cannot claim absolute finality for a dogma without claiming a commensurate finality for the sphere of thought within which it arose. If the dogmas of the Christian Church from the second to the sixth centuries express finally and sufficiently the truths concerning the topics about which they deal, then the Greek philosophy of that period had developed a system of ideas of equal finality. You cannot limit the inspiration to a narrow circle of creeds.

A dogma—in the sense of a precise statement—can never be final; it can only be adequate in its adjustment of certain abstract concepts. But the estimate of the status of these concepts remains for determination.

You cannot rise above the adequacy of the terms you employ. A dogma may be true in the sense that it expresses such interrelations of the subject matter as are expressible within the set of ideas employed. But if the same dogma be used intolerantly so as to check the employment of other modes of analyzing the subject matter, then, for all its truth, it will be doing the work of a falsehood.

Progress in truth—truth of science and truth of religion—is mainly a progress in the framing of concepts, in discarding artificial abstractions or partial metaphors, and in evolving notions which strike more deeply into the root of reality.

2. EXPERIENCE AND EXPRESSION

Expression is the one fundamental sacrament. It is the outward and visible sign of an inward and spiritual grace. It follows that, in the process of forming a common expression of direct intuition, there is first a stage of primary expression into some medium of sense-experience which each individual contributes at first hand. No one can do this for another. It is the contribution of each to the knowledge of all.

This primary expression mainly clothes itself in the media of action and of words, but also partly of art. Their expressiveness to others arises from the fact that they are interpretable in terms of the intuitions of the recipients. Apart from such interpretation, the modes of expression remain accidental, unrationalized happenings of mere sense-experience; but with such interpretation, the recipient extends his apprehension of the ordered universe by penetrating into the inward nature of the originator of the expression. There is then a community of intuition by reason of the sacrament of expression proffered by one and received by the other.

But the expressive sign is more than interpretable. It is creative. It elicits the intuition which interprets it. It cannot elicit what is not there. A note on a tuning fork can elicit a response from a piano. But the piano has already in it the string tuned to the same note. In the same way the expressive sign elicits the existent intuition which would not otherwise emerge into individual distinctiveness. Again in theological language, the sign works *ex opere operato*, but only within the limitation that the recipient be patient of the creative action.

There is very little really first-hand expression in the world. By this I mean that most expression is what may be termed responsive expression, namely, expression which expresses intuitions elicited by the expressions of others. This is as it should be; since in this way what is permanent, important, and widely spread, receives more and more a clear definition.

But there is need for something more than this responsive expression. For it is not true that there is easy apprehension of the great formative generalities. They are embedded under the rubbish of irrelevant detail. Men knew a lot about dogs before they thought of backbones and of vertebrates. The great intuitions, which in their respective provinces set all things right, dawn but slowly upon history.

With this prevalence of responsive expression, we are used to a learned literature and to imitative conduct. When we get anything which is neither learned nor imitative, it is often very evil. But sometimes it is genius.

The history of culture shows that originality of expression is not a process of continuous development. There are antecedent periods of slow evolution. Finally, as if touched by a spark, a very few persons, one, two, or three, in some particular province of experience, express completely novel intuitions. Such intuitions can be responded to, analyzed in terms of their relationships to other ideas, fused with other forms of experience, but as individual primary intuitions within their own province of experience they are not surpassed.

The world will not repeat Dante, Shakespeare, Socrates, or the Greek tragedians. These men, in connection with the tiny groups forming their immediate environments of associates and successors and perhaps of equals, add something once and for all. We develop in connection with them, but not beyond them, in respect to those definite intuitions which they flashed upon the world. These examples are taken from the circle of literature merely for the sake of easy intelligibility.

There are two points to be noticed about them. In the first place, they are associated with a small stage fitted for their peculiar originality. Standardized size can do almost anything, except foster the growth of genius.

That is the privilege of the tiny oasis. Goethe surveyed the world, but it was from Weimar; Shakespeare is universal, but he lived in Elizabethan England. We cannot think of Socrates outside Athens.

The second characteristic is that their peculiar originality is the very element in their expression which remains unformularized. They deal with what all men know, and they make it new. They do not bring to the world a new formula nor do they discover new facts, but in expressing their apprehensions of the world, they leave behind them an element of novelty—a new expression forever evoking its proper response.

Some original men do express themselves in formulae: but the formula then expresses something beyond itself. The formula is then secondary to its meaning; it is, in a sense, a literary device. The formula sinks in importance, or even is abandoned; but its meaning remains fructifying in the world, finding new expression to suit new circumstances. The formula was not wrong, but it was limited to its own sphere of thought.

In particular, the view that there are a few

fundamental dogmas is arbitrary. Every true dogma which formulates with some adequacy the facts of a complex religious experience is fundamental for the individual in question and he disregards it at his peril. For formulation increases vividness of apprehension, and the peril is the loss of an aid in the difficult task of spiritual ascent.

But every individual suffers from invincible ignorance; and a dogma which fails to evoke any response in immediate apprehension stifles the religious life. There is no mechanical rule and no escape from the necessity of complete sincerity either way.

Thus religion is primarily individual, and the dogmas of religion are clarifying modes of external expression. The intolerant use of religious dogmas has practically destroyed their utility for a great, if not the greater part, of the civilized world.

Expression, and in particular expression by dogma, is the return from solitariness to society. There is no such thing as absolute solitariness. Each entity requires its environment. Thus man cannot seclude himself from society.

Even for individual intuitions outward expression is necessary, as a sacrament in which the minister and recipient are one. But further, what is known in secret must be enjoyed in common, and must be verified in common. The immediate conviction of the moment in this way justifies itself as a rational principle enlightening the objective world.

The great instantaneous conviction in this way becomes the Gospel, the good news. It insists on its universality, because it is either that or a passing fancy. The conversion of the Gentiles is both the effect of truth and the test of truth.

Thus the simplicity of inspiration has passed from its first expression into responsive experience. It then disengages itself from particular experience by formulation in precise dogmas, and so faces the transformations of history.

In this passage a religion coalesces with other factors in human life. It is expanded, explained, modified, adapted. If it was originally founded upon truth, it maintains its identity by its recurrence to the inspired simplicity of its origin. The dogmas are statements of how the complex world is to be expressed in the light of the intuitions fundamental to the religion. They are not necessarily simple in character or limited in number.

3. THE THREE TRADITIONS

The divergence in the expression of dogmas is most clearly shown in the two traditions of Buddhism and Christianity. This divergence is important because it reaches down to the most fundamental religious concepts, namely, the nature of God, and the aim of life.

There are close analogies between the two religions. In both there is, in some sense, a saviour—Christ in the one, and the Buddha in the other. But their functions differ, according to the theologies of the two religions. In both, the souls of the blessed return to God. Again, this analogy cloaks a wide divergence; for the respective concepts of God, and the respective concepts of the meaning of the return of the soul, differ in both cases.

The moral codes have striking analogies. But again there are divergencies which flow naturally from the theological differences. To put it briefly, Buddhism, on the whole, discourages the sense of active personality, whereas Christianity encourages it. For example, modern European philosophy, which had its origin in Plato and Aristotle, after sixteen hundred years of Christianity reformulated its problems with increased attention to the importance of the individual subject of experience, conceived as an abiding entity with a transition of experiences. If Europe, after the Greek period, had been subject to the Buddhist religion, the change of philosophical climate would have been in the other direction.

This reformation of philosophy has emphasized the divergence. For the abiding individual substance, mind or matter, is now conceived as the subject supporting the transition of experiences. Thus, according to prevalent Western notions, the moral aims of Buddhism are directed to altering the first principles of metaphysics.

The absolute idealism, so influential in Europe and America during the last third of the nineteenth century, and still powerful notwithstanding the reaction from it, was undoubtedly a reaction towards Buddhistic metaphysics on the part of the Western mentality. The multiplicity of finite enduring individuals were relegated to a world of appearances, and the ultimate reality was centred in an Absolute.

But meanwhile science had appeared as a third organized system of thought which in many respects played the part of a theology, by reason of the answers which it gave to current theological questions. Science suggested a cosmology; and whatever suggests a cosmology, suggests a religion.

From its very beginning in the sixteenth and seventeenth centuries, science emphasized ideas which modified the religious picture of the world. As the medieval picture dissolved, religion and philosophy equally received shock after shock, with a final culmination in the middle of the nineteenth century.

Philosophy, by its nature, was less wedded

to its aboriginal picture of the world than was religion. Accordingly it divided itself into two streams of thought. One stream subordinated itself entirely to science, and has asserted its mission to be the discussion of the proper coördination of notions employed in current scientific practice. The other stream, which is that of absolute idealism, sidetracked science by proclaiming that science dealt with finite truths respecting a world of appearances; and that these appearances were not very real, and that these truths were not very true. It reserved for philosophy the determination of all that was to be known concerning the ultimate reality, and concerning our own participation in that final absolute fact.

The importance of rational religion in the history of modern culture is that it stands or falls with its fundamental position, that we know more than can be formulated in one finite systematized scheme of abstractions, however important that scheme may be in the elucidation of some aspect of the order of things.

The final principle of religion is that there

is a wisdom in the nature of things, from which flow our direction of practice, and our possibility of the theoretical analysis of fact. It grounds this principle upon two sources of evidence, first upon our success in various special theoretical sciences, physical and otherwise; and secondly, upon our knowledge of a discernment of ordered relationships, especially in aesthetic valuations, which stretches far beyond anything which has been expressed systematically in words.

According to religion, this discernment of relationships forms in itself the very substance of existence. The formulations are the froth upon the surface. Religion insists that the world is a mutually adjusted disposition of things, issuing in value for its own sake. This is the very point that science is always forgetting.

Religions commit suicide when they find their inspirations in their dogmas. The inspiration of religion lies in the history of religion. By this I mean that it is to be found in the primary expressions of the intuitions of the finest types of religious lives. The sources of religious belief are always growing, though some supreme expressions may lie in the past. Records of these sources are not formulae. They elicit in us intuitive response which pierces beyond dogma.

But dogmatic expression is necessary. For whatever has objective validity is capable of partial expression in terms of abstract concepts, so that a coherent doctrine arises which elucidates the world beyond the locus of the origin of the dogmas in question.

Also exact statements are the media by which identical intuitions into the world can be identified amid a wide variety of circumstances.

But the dogmas, however true, are only bits of the truth, expressed in terms which in some ways are over-assertive and in other ways lose the essence of truth. When exactly understood in relation to an exact system of philosophic thought, they may—or may not —be exactly true.

But in respect to this exact truth, they are very abstract—much more abstract than the representations of them in popular thought. Also in fact, there never has been any exact, complete system of philosophic thought, and there never has been any exact understanding of dogmas, an understanding which has been properly confined to strict interpretation in terms of a philosophic system, complete or incomplete.

Accordingly, though dogmas have their measure of truth, which is unalterable, in their precise forms they are narrow, limitative, and alterable: in effect untrue, when carried over beyond the proper scope of their utility.

A system of dogmas may be the ark within which the Church floats safely down the flood-tide of history. But the Church will perish unless it opens its window and lets out the dove to search for an olive branch. Sometimes even it will do well to disembark on Mount Ararat and build a new altar to the divine Spirit—an altar neither in Mount Gerizim nor yet at Jerusalem.

The decay of Christianity and Buddhism, as determinative influences in modern thought, is partly due to the fact that each religion has unduly sheltered itself from the other. The self-sufficient pedantry of learning and the confidence of ignorant zealots have combined to shut up each religion in its own forms of thought. Instead of looking to each other for deeper meanings, they have remained self-satisfied and unfertilized.

Both have suffered from the rise of the third tradition, which is science, because neither of them had retained the requisite flexibility of adaptation. Thus the real, practical problems of religion have never been adequately studied in the only way in which such problems *can* be studied, namely, in the school of experience.

One most obvious problem is how to save the intermediate imaginative representations of spiritual truths from loss of effectiveness, if the possibility of modifications of dogma are admitted. The religious spirit is not identical with dialectical acuteness. Thus these intermediate representations play a great part in religious life. They are enshrined in modes of worship, in popular religious literature, and in art. Religions cannot do without them; but if they are allowed to dominate, uncriticised by dogma or by recurrence to the primary sources of religious inspiration, they are properly to be termed idols. In Christian

history, the charge of idolatry has been ban-
died to and fro among rival theologians. Probably, if taken in its wide sense, it rests with
equal truth on all the main churches, Protes-
tant and Catholic. Idolatry is the necessary
product of static dogmas.

But the problem of so handling popular
forms of thought as to keep their full reference to the primary sources, and yet also to
keep them in touch with the best critical dogmas of their times, is no easy one. The chief
figures in the history of the Christian Church
who seem to have grasped explicitly its central importance were, Origen in the Church
of Alexandria, in the early part of the third
century, and Erasmus in the early part of the
sixteenth century. Their analogous fates show
the wavering attitude of the Christian Church,
culminating in lapses into dogmatic idolatry.
It must, however, be assigned to the great
credit of the Papacy of his time, that Erasmus never in his lifetime lost the support of
the court of Rome.* Unfortunately Erasmus,

* Erasmus received the offer of a Cardinalate in 1534,
and died in 1536; his works have since been placed on
the Index.

though a good man, was no hero, and the moral atmosphere of the Renaissance Papacy was not equal to its philosophic insight. In the phrase of Leo X, the quarrel of monks began; and yet another golden opportunity was lost, while rival pedants cut out neat little dogmatic systems to serve as the unalterable measure of the Universe.

4. THE NATURE OF GOD

The general history of religious thought, of which the Reformation period is a particular instance, is that of the endeavour of mankind to interpret the great standard experiences as leading to a more definite knowledge than can be derived from a metaphysic which founds itself upon general experience.

There can be nothing inherently illegitimate in such an attempt. But if we attend to the general principles which regulate all endeavours after clear statement of truth, we must be prepared to amplify, recast, generalize, and adapt, so as to absorb into one system all sources of experience.

The earlier statements will be not so much wrong, as obscured by trivial limitations, and as thereby implying an exclusion of complementary truths. The growth will be in the proportion of truth.

The doctrines—fundamental to religion—of the nature of God must be construed in this sense. It is in respect to this doctrine that the great cleavages of religious thought arise. The extremes are the doctrine of God as the impersonal order of the universe, and the doctrine of God as the one person creating the universe.

A general concept has to be construed in terms of a descriptive metaphysical system. In this concluding section of this course, we ask what can be said of the nature of God in terms of the metaphysical description which has been adopted as the basis of thought in this course of lectures, and which was more particularly described in the previous lecture.

To be an actual thing is to be limited. An actual thing is an elicited feeling-value, which is analyzable as the outcome of a graded grasping of the elements of the universe into the unity of one fact. This grasping together may be called a perception. The grading means the grading of relevance of the various elements, so far as concerns their contribution to the one actual fact.

The synthesis is the union of what is already actual with what is, for that occasion, new for realization. I have called it the union of the actual ground with the novel consequent. The ground is formed by all the facts of the world, already actual and graded in their proportion of relevance. The consequent is constituted by all the ideal forms of possibility, graded in their proportion. The grading of the actual ground arises from the creativity of some actual fact passing over into a new form by reason of the fact itself. The new creativity, under consideration, has thus already a definite status in the world, arising from its particular origin. We can indifferently say that the grading arises from the status, or the status from the grading. They are different ways of saying the same thing.

The grading of the ideal forms arises from

the grading of the actual facts. It is the union
of the forms with the facts in such measure
as to elicit a renewed feeling-value, of the
type possible as a novel outcome from the
antecedent facts.

Depth of value is only possible if the antecedent facts conspire in unison. Thus a measure of harmony in the ground is requisite
for the perpetuation of depth into the future.
But harmony is limitation. Thus rightness of
limitation is essential for growth of reality.

Unlimited possibility and abstract creativity can procure nothing. The limitation,
and the basis arising from what is already
actual, are both of them necessary and inter-
connected.

Thus the whole process itself, viewed at
any stage as a definite limited fact which has
issued from the creativity, requires a definite
entity, already actual among the formative
elements, as an antecedent ground for the
entry of the ideal forms into the definite process of the temporal world.

But such a complete aboriginal actuality
must differ from actuality in process of realization in respect to the blind occasions of

perceptivity which issue from process and require process. These occasions build up the physical world which is essentially in transition.

God, who is the ground antecedent to transition, must include all possibilities of physical value conceptually, thereby holding the ideal forms apart in equal, conceptual realization of knowledge. Thus, as concepts, they are grasped together in the synthesis of omniscience.

The limitation of God is his goodness. He gains his depth of actuality by his harmony of valuation. It is not true that God is in all respects infinite. If He were, He would be evil as well as good. Also this unlimited fusion of evil with good would mean mere nothingness. He is something decided and is thereby limited.

He is complete in the sense that his vision determines every possibility of value. Such a complete vision coördinates and adjusts every detail. Thus his knowledge of the relationships of particular modes of value is not added to, or disturbed, by the realization in the actual world of what is already conceptually realized in his ideal world. This ideal world of conceptual harmonization is merely a description of God himself. Thus the nature of God is the complete conceptual realization of the realm of ideal forms. The kingdom of heaven is God. But these forms are not realized by him in mere bare isolation, but as elements in the value of his conceptual experience. Also, the ideal forms are in God's vision as contributing to his complete experience, by reason of his conceptual realization of their possibilities as elements of value in any creature. Thus God is the one systematic, complete fact, which is the antecedent ground conditioning every creative act.

The depths of his existence lie beyond the vulgarities of praise or of power. He gives to suffering its swift insight into values which can issue from it. He is the ideal companion who transmutes what has been lost into a living fact within his own nature. He is the mirror which discloses to every creature its own greatness.

The kingdom of heaven is not the isolation of good from evil. It is the overcoming of evil by good. This transmutation of evil into good enters into the actual world by reason of the inclusion of the nature of God, which includes the ideal vision of each actual evil so met with a novel consequent as to issue in the restoration of goodness.

God has in his nature the knowledge of evil, of pain, and of degradation, but it is there as overcome with what is good. Every fact is what it is, a fact of pleasure, of joy, of pain, or of suffering. In its union with God that fact is not a total loss, but on its finer side is an element to be woven immortally into the rhythm of mortal things. Its very evil becomes a stepping stone in the all-embracing ideals of God.

Every event on its finer side introduces God into the world. Through it his ideal vision is given a base in actual fact to which He provides the ideal consequent, as a factor saving the world from the self-destruction of evil. The power by which God sustains the world is the power of himself as the ideal. He adds himself to the actual ground from which every creative act takes its rise. The world lives by its incarnation of God in itself.

He transcends the temporal world, because He is an actual fact in the nature of things. He is not there as derivative from the world; He is the actual fact from which the other formative elements cannot be torn apart.

But equally it stands in his nature that He is the realization of the ideal conceptual harmony by reason of which there is an actual process in the total universe—an evolving world which is actual because there is order.

The abstract forms are thus the link between God and the actual world. These forms are abstract and not real, because in themselves they represent no achievement of actual value. Actual fact always means fusion into one perceptivity. God is one such conceptual fusion, embracing the concept of all such possibilities graded in harmonious, relative subordination. Each actual occasion in the temporal world is another such fusion. The forms belong no more to God than to any one occasion. Apart from these forms, no rational description can be given either of God or of the actual world. Apart from God, there would be no actual world; and apart from the actual world with its creativity, there would be no rational explanation of the ideal vision which constitutes God.

Each actual occasion gives to the creativity which flows from it a definite character in two ways. In one way, as a fact, enjoying its complex of relationships with the rest of the world, it contributes a ground—partly good and partly bad—for the creativity to fuse with a novel consequent, which will be the outcome of its free urge. In another way, as transmuted in the nature of God, the ideal consequent as it stands in his vision is also added. Thus God in the world is the perpetual vision of the road which leads to the deeper realities.

5. CONCLUSION

God is that function in the world by reason of which our purposes are directed to ends which in our own consciousness are impartial as to our own interests. He is that element in life in virtue of which judgment stretches beyond facts of existence to values of existence. He is that element in virtue of which our purposes extend beyond values for ourselves to values for others. He is that element in virtue of which the attainment of such a value for others transforms itself into value for ourselves.

He is the binding element in the world. The consciousness which is individual in us, is universal in him: the love which is partial in us is all-embracing in him. Apart from him there could be no world, because there could be no adjustment of individuality. His purpose in the world is quality of attainment. His purpose is always embodied in the particular ideals relevant to the actual state of the world. Thus all attainment is immortal in that it fashions the actual ideals which are God in the world as it is now. Every act leaves the world with a deeper or a fainter impress of God. He then passes into his next relation to the world with enlarged, or diminished, presentation of ideal values.

He is not the world, but the valuation of the world. In abstraction from the course of events, this valuation is a necessary metaphysical function. Apart from it, there could be no definite determination of limitation required for attainment. But in the actual world, He confronts what is actual in it with what is possible for it. Thus He solves all indeterminations.

The passage of time is the journey of the world towards the gathering of new ideas into actual fact. This adventure is upwards and downwards. Whatever ceases to ascend, fails to preserve itself and enters upon its inevitable path of decay. It decays by transmitting its nature to slighter occasions of actuality, by reason of the failure of the new forms to fertilize the perceptive achievements which constitute its past history. The universe shows us two aspects: on one side it is physically wasting, on the other side it is spiritually ascending.

It is thus passing with a slowness, inconceivable in our measures of time, to new creative conditions, amid which the physical world, as we at present know it, will be represented by a ripple barely to be distinguished from nonentity.

The present type of order in the world has arisen from an unimaginable past, and it will find its grave in an unimaginable future. There remain the inexhaustible realm of abstract forms, and creativity, with its shifting character ever determined afresh by its own creatures, and God, upon whose wisdom all forms of order depend.

ALFRED NORTH WHITEHEAD

Philosopher and mathematician, Alfred North Whitehead was born in 1861 in Ramsgate, Kent, the son of an English pastor. He was educated at Trinity College, Cambridge University, and from 1914 to 1924 he was professor and dean of the faculty at the Imperial College of Science and Technology at the University of London. In 1924 he became professor of philosophy at Harvard University. In collaboration with Bertrand Russell, he wrote the now classic PRINCIPIA MATHEMATICA. *Among his many works of philosophy are* PROCESS AND REALITY, SCIENCE AND THE MODERN WORLD, ADVENTURES OF IDEAS, SYMBOLISM, *and* MODES OF THOUGHT. THE AIMS OF EDUCATION *and the present work*, RELIGION IN THE MAKING, *reflect Whitehead's abiding interest in bringing to bear on modern culture the temperate and judicious findings of philosophic speculation. Alfred North Whitehead died in 1947.*

MERIDIAN BOOKS

Religion (General)

BARTH, KARL *Anselm: Fides Quaerens Intellectum (Faith in Search of Understanding)*. LA39

BOUYER, LOUIS *Newman*. M87

CAMPBELL, JOSEPH *The Hero with a Thousand Faces*. M22

COGLEY, JOHN (ED.) *Religion in America*. M60

DANIÉLOU, JEAN *God and the Ways of Knowing*. M96

D'ARCY, M. C. *The Mind and Heart of Love*. M26

D'ARCY, M. C., GILSON, ETIENNE, ET AL. *St. Augustine: His Age, Life, and Thought*. M51

DAWSON, CHRISTOPHER *Religion and Culture*. M53

DRIVER, S. R. *An Introduction to the Literature of the Old Testament*. MG29

DUPONT-SOMMER, A. *The Essene Writings from Qumran*. MG44

HAZELTON, ROGER (ED.) *Selected Writings of St. Augustine*. LA37

LIETZMANN, HANS *A History of the Early Church, Vol. I*. MG26A

LIETZMANN, HANS *A History of the Early Church, Vol. II*. MG26B

MARITAIN, JACQUES *St. Thomas Aquinas*. M55

MILLER, PERRY *Jonathan Edwards*. M75

PIKE, E. ROYSTON *Encyclopaedia of Religion and Religions*. MG37

REINHOLD, H. A. (ED.) *The Soul Afire*. MG28

SMITH, W. ROBERTSON *The Religion of the Semites*. ML4

UNDERHILL, EVELYN *Mysticism*. MG1

WELLHAUSEN, JULIUS *Prolegomena to the History of Ancient Israel*. MG35

WHITE, VICTOR *God and the Unconscious*. M120

WHITEHEAD, ALFRED NORTH *Religion in the Making*. LA28

WILSON, EDMUND *The Scrolls from the Dead Sea*. M69

Meridian Books are published by The World Publishing Company, Cleveland and New York. For a free Meridian catalogue write to Dept. AM, Meridian Books, 119 West 57th Street, N.Y.

MERIDIAN BOOKS

Of Catholic Interest

BOUYER, LOUIS *Newman.* M87

BROWNE, E. MARTIN (ED.) *Religious Drama 2: Mystery and Morality Plays.* LA20

COGLEY, JOHN (ED.) *Religion in America.* M60

DANIÉLOU, JEAN *God and the Ways of Knowing.* M96

D'ARCY, M. C. *The Meaning and Matter of History.* M110

D'ARCY, M. C. *The Mind and Heart of Love.* M26

D'ARCY, M. C., GILSON, ETIENNE, ET AL. *St. Augustine: His Age, Life, and Thought.* M51

DAWSON, CHRISTOPHER *The Making of Europe.* M35

DAWSON, CHRISTOPHER *Religion and Culture.* M53

GUARDINI, ROMANO *The Death of Socrates.* M138

HASKINS, C. H. *The Renaissance of the 12th Century.* M49

HAZELTON, ROGER (ED.) *Selected Writings of St. Augustine.* LA37

MARITAIN, JACQUES *Creative Intuition in Art and Poetry.* M8

MARITAIN, JACQUES *St. Thomas Aquinas.* M55

MARTY, MARTIN E. *A Short History of Christianity.* LA24

REINHOLD, H. A. *The Soul Afire.* MG28

VIGNAUX, PAUL *Philosophy in the Middle Ages.* M81

WHITE, VICTOR *God and the Unconscious.* M120

Meridian Books are published by The World Publishing Company, Cleveland and New York. For a free Meridian catalogue write to Dept. AM, Meridian Books, 119 West 57th Street, N.Y.

MERIDIAN BOOKS

Of Protestant Interest (Living Age Books)

BARTH, KARL *Anselm: Fides Quaerens Intellectum (Faith in Search of Understanding).* LA39

BARTH, KARL *The Faith of the Church.* LA22

BERDYAEV, NICHOLAS *Dostoevsky.* LA15

BERDYAEV, NICHOLAS *The Meaning of History.* LA36

BOEHMER, HEINRICH *Martin Luther: Road to Reformation.* LA9

BRIGHTMAN, F. E. (ED.) *The Private Devotions of Lancelot Andrewes.* LA32

BROWNE, E. MARTIN *Religious Drama 2: Mystery and Morality Plays.* LA20

BULTMANN, RUDOLF *Primitive Christianity in Its Contemporary Setting.* LA4

BURROWS, MILLAR *What Mean These Stones?* LA7

CULLMANN, OSCAR *Peter: Disciple, Apostle, Martyr.* LA21

DODD, C. H. *The Meaning of Paul for Today.* LA8

FEY, HAROLD E. (ED.) *How My Mind Has Changed.* LA33

GILL, THEODORE (ED.) *The Sermons of John Donne.* LA17

HALVERSON, MARVIN (ED.) *Religious Drama 1: Five Plays.* LA10

HALVERSON, MARVIN (ED.) *Religious Drama 3.* LA27

HALVERSON, MARVIN, AND COHEN, ARTHUR A. (EDS.) *A Handbook of Christian Theology.* LA18

HAZELTON, ROGER (ED.) *Selected Writings of St. Augustine.* LA37

HOLL, KARL *The Cultural Significance of the Reformation.* LA25

INGE, W. R. *Christian Mysticism.* LA3

LEFEVER, ERNEST; MORGENTHAU, HANS (INTRO.) *Ethics and United States Foreign Policy.* LA19

MARTY, MARTIN E. *The Infidel: Freethought and American Religion.* LA34

MARTY, MARTIN E. *A Short History of Christianity.* LA24

NIEBUHR, H. RICHARD *The Social Sources of Denominationalism.* LA11

NIEBUHR, REINHOLD *An Interpretation of Christian Ethics.* LA1

NIEBUHR, REINHOLD *Essays in Applied Christianity.* LA26

NIEBUHR, REINHOLD *Leaves from the Notebooks of a Tamed Cynic.* LA13

NOSS, LUTHER (ED.) *Christian Hymns.* LA38

OESTERLEY, W. O. E., AND ROBINSON, THEODORE H. *An Introduction to the Books of the Old Testament.* LA23

OGDEN, SCHUBERT M. (ED.) *Existence and Faith: Shorter Writings of Rudolf Bultmann.* LA29

OTTO, RUDOLF *Mysticism East and West.* LA14

ROWLEY, H. H. *The Unity of the Bible.* LA16

SAYERS, DOROTHY L. *The Mind of the Maker.* LA2

TALON, HENRI A. *God's Knotty Log: Selected Writings of John Bunyan.* LA31

THOMPSON, BARD (ED.) *Liturgies of the Western Church.* LA35

TILLICH, PAUL *The Religious Situation.* LA6

TROELTSCH, ERNEST *Christian Thought.* LA12

VISSER 'T HOOFT, W. A. *Rembrandt and the Gospel.* LA30

WHITEHEAD, ALFRED NORTH *Religion in the Making.* LA28

WILLIAMS, CHARLES *The Descent of the Dove.* LA5

Meridian Books are published by The World Publishing Company, Cleveland and New York. For a free Meridian catalogue write to Dept. AM, Meridian Books, 119 West 57th Street, N.Y.